RAMSES II

RAMSES II

Ramses II:
The Pharaoh and His Time
Exhibition Catalog
Brigham Young University
25 October 1985 to
5 April 1986

Lisa K. Sabbahy, Historical
Background and
Object Descriptions
C. Wilfred Griggs, Editor
Kenneth S. Graetz, City of
Montréal, Exhibit Photography

For additional copies write to
RAMSES II
Brigham Young University
205 UPB
Provo, UT 84602

$8 per copy plus $2 handling and shipping

ISBN 0-8425-2206-9

CONTENTS

Under the distinguished patronage
of His Excellency,
Mr. Hosni Mubarak, President of
the Arab Republic of Egypt

His Excellency, the Prime
Minister of the Arab Republic of
Egypt, Dr. Ali Lutfi

His Excellency, the Minister of
Foreign Affairs of
the Arab Republic of Egypt,
Dr. Ahmed Esmat Abd el-Meguid

His Excellency, the Minister of
Culture of the Arab Republic of
Egypt, Dr. Ahmed Haikal

His Excellency, the Ambassador
of the Arab Republic of Egypt
to the United States,
Mr. Abd el-Aal Raouf el-Reidy

His Excellency, the Ambassador
of the Arab Republic of Egypt,
Consul General of San Francisco,
Mr. Ismail Abd el-Moeti

His Excellency, the First Under
Secretary of State of the Arab
Republic of Egypt and Chairman,
Egyptian Antiquities
Organization, Dr. Ahmed Kadry

His Excellency, the former
Chairman of the Egyptian
Antiquities Organization and
member of its Board of Directors,
Dr. Gamal El-Din Mokhtar

The Director General of Egyptian
Museums, Egyptian
Antiquities Organization,
Mr. Ibrahim el-Nawawy

The Director General of Technical
Affairs of Egyptian Museums,
Mr. Mohamed Ahmed Mohsen

The Director General of the
Egyptian Museum, Cairo,
Dr. Mohamed Saleh

Dr. Ahmed Kadry
Chairman, Egyptian Antiquities
Organization

Mr. Ibrahim el-Nawawy
Director General of Egyptian
Museums, Egyptian Antiquities
Organization

Mr. Mohamed Ahmed Mohsen
Director General of Technical
Affairs of Egyptian Museums

Dr. Mohamed Saleh
Director General of the Egyptian
Museum, Cairo

Dr. Abdel-Aziz Sadek
Assistant Director General of the
Center for Documentation on
Ancient Egypt

Mrs. Saneya Abd el-Aal
Assistant Director of the Egyptian
Museum, Cairo

Mr. Galal Sharawy
Assistant Director of the Egyptian
Museum, Cairo

A Message from the Chairman

This exhibit of pieces from the time of the Egyptian pharaoh Ramses II at Brigham Young University in Utah forms a bridge of civilization between Egypt and the United States. The Egyptian Antiquities Organization accepted Brigham Young University's invitation to exhibit this show after its successful exhibition in Montréal, Canada, to strengthen cultural ties between the Egyptian government and Brigham Young University.

Ramses II was one of ancient Egypt's greatest rulers. Because of the enormous number of his buildings, this king has made Egypt a large open-air museum. Ramses II not only built the temples at Abu Simbel, well known to Americans, but he also added to the temples at Luxor, Karnak, Abydos, Memphis, and the Ramesside capital at Pi-Ramses in the eastern Delta.

The pieces in this show give a very clear impression of ancient Egyptian civilization in the thirteenth century, B.C. We are sure that this exhibition is going to strengthen the relationship between the people of Egypt and the state of Utah and surrounding states. The Egyptian Antiquities Organization hopes that this cultural sharing increases cooperation between the peoples of Egypt and America in many endeavors.

First Under Secretary of State, Chairman, Egyptian Antiquities Organization

Dr. Ahmed Kadry

Ramses II:
The Pharaoh and His Time
25 October 1985 to 5 April 1986

Hosted by
Brigham Young University,
a private university sponsored by
The Church of Jesus Christ of
Latter-day Saints

Administration
Jeffrey R. Holland, President
Jae R. Ballif, Provost and Academic
Vice-President
John B. Stohlton, Executive Vice-
President
Dee F. Andersen, Administrative
Vice-President

Project Director
C. Wilfred Griggs with Special
Assistance and Collaboration from
Fattah Sabbahy

Executive Committee
Jae R. Ballif, Provost and Academic
Vice-President
John B. Stohlton, Executive Vice-
President
Dee F. Andersen, Administrative
Vice-President
C. Wilfred Griggs, Director of
Ancient Studies
George H. Bowie, Executive
Director of Public Affairs
Robert J. Matthews, Dean of
Religious Education
Ray C. Hillam, Director of the
David M. Kennedy Center for
International Studies

Operations Committee
Sue Bergin
Douglas C. Cox
Norman A. Darais
Richard C. Eddy
Dean Fairbank
Connie B. Gaither
Richard K. Grover
Wayne J. Lott
McRay Magleby
Wm. Revell Phillips
Paul C. Richards
J. Wesley Sherwood
John L. Sorenson
Scott Williams

Museum Preparation
J. Clyff Allen
Dorald M. Allred
Karren B. Barley
Clark B. Brereton
Douglas C. Cox
George Homsey
Kenneth W. Packer
Richard C. Weiss

Publicity and Marketing
Sue Bergin
George H. Bowie
Norma G. Collett
Mark A. Philbrick
Paul C. Richards
Hal Gardiner and Associates

Physical Facilities
Edwin Cozzens
Warren J. Jones
Byron Paulsen Construction,
Contractor

Exhibit Catalog
Lisa K. Sabbahy, Historical
Background and
Object Descriptions
C. Wilfred Griggs, Editor
Kenneth S. Graetz, City of
Montréal, Exhibit Photography
Norman A. Darais,
Production Editor
Judy B. Garvin and Karen Seely,
Copy Editors
McRay Magleby and
Linda Sullivan, Design
Brian Bean and John Snyder,
Graphic Production
Gordon C. Lonsdale and
W. Grant Williams—BYU Motion
Picture Studio, Area Photography
Richard K. Grover and
West A. Barton, Printing
Production

Special thanks to:
The Honorable Orrin G. Hatch,
United States Senate
Esherick, Homsey, Dodge, and
Davis, Architects and Planners,
San Francisco, California

It is fitting to begin an introduction to ancient Egypt with a brief description of the Nile River, for it has often been said that "Egypt is a gift of the Nile." This river, which flows through the entire length of Egypt, originates much farther to the south. The Blue Nile rises in the Ethiopian highlands, and the White Nile flows from the waters of Lake Victoria. Near modern Khartoum in the Sudan, these two rivers join to become the Nile, which then flows north through Egypt to the Mediterranean.

Just north of Cairo the Nile splits into branches, spreading out to form the Egyptian Delta. Two distinct parts of Egypt are thus formed by the river: the long, narrow valley in the south, or Upper Egypt, and the Delta in the north, or Lower Egypt. To the Egyptian mind, Egypt has always been composed of these two parts. In fact, ancient Egyptian kings were called "King of Upper and Lower Egypt." Another common epithet applied to the king was "Lord of the Two Lands," again referring to Upper and Lower Egypt.

The difference in terrain and appearance between these two parts of Egypt is quite dramatic. In Upper Egypt the arable land is limited to narrow strips averaging eight miles wide along the river. The river valley is flanked by the cliffs that begin the high desert plateaus on the east and west. On the other hand, in the Delta, the river spreads out over a hundred miles, and the region is wide, flat, and lush.

Approximately 25,000 B.C. the Blue Nile and the White Nile joined into one river, bringing about the pattern of annual flooding that deposited a thin layer of silt on Egypt's entire river valley. The river began to rise in the early summer, and, until the fall, the land on both sides of the river was covered with water that both irrigated and deposited fertilizing silt. The waters then slowly receded, until at the end of spring the Nile was low. It was during the eight-month period of receding and low waters that Egyptians repeated the process of surveying and preparing the silt-enriched soil, planting, irrigating, and harvesting their crops. This ancient pattern of the Nile and its agricultural cycle did not cease or markedly change until the completion of the Aswan High Dam in 1971.

By 4000 B.C. Neolithic man had settled in small communities in the Nile Valley. These early people had by then begun to grow emmer and barley, to domesticate sheep and goats, and to produce pottery. They had long since mastered the techniques of manufacturing stone tools. Each settlement apparently had its ruling chieftain and its own cult, or local divinity. As time went on certain of these communities became more important, dominating the others. One causative factor was that some settlements, located at the end of trade routes, became economically powerful. As an area grew in importance, so did its religious cult, and particular gods thus became more important than others.

Eventually, between 3100 and 3000 B.C., a ruler from Upper Egypt attacked and conquered Lower Egypt, uniting the country. Narmer, whose slate palette in the Cairo Museum depicts him as victorious over Lower Egypt, was probably this ruler. At this time a number of other changes also took place. First (and foremost in importance for modern scholars), the Egyptians began to leave written records, using the writing system we call ancient Egyptian hieroglyphs. Thus Egypt entered into the "historical period" (so designated by the appearance of written materials), with King Narmer the first king of the First Dynasty. In all, Egypt was ruled by thirty-one dynasties, the last of which ended when Alexander the Great, who took Egypt in 332 B.C., died.

With the First and Second dynasties, a time scholars refer to as the Early Dynastic Period, the basic elements of ancient Egyptian culture were formed: religious beliefs, mythology, kingship, government structure, and the beginnings of monumental art and architecture. All these facets of ancient Egypt developed or were refined with time, but the concepts and traditions behind them were unchanging. In fact, ancient Egypt's most remarkable aspect is that its culture persisted for almost three thousand years with relatively little change; the very nature of ancient Egyptian culture was static.

In modern Western societies innovation and change are viewed positively. Ancient Egyptians held an opposite point of view, for they believed that in the very beginning the universe and universal order had been permanently established. It was exactly this way, the way it had been set down on the so-called "First Occasion," that everything should remain. In the beginning everything had been established according to *Ma'at*, "truth" or "justice." Ma'at governed nature, as well as the life of the gods and men. In order that the universe function properly and the gods be satisfied, which in turn brought well-being to man, it was imperative that the king rule according to Ma'at. This was perhaps the king's most important responsibility.

Memphis, the capital of ancient Egypt, was founded at the beginning of the First Dynasty. It was located just southwest of modern Cairo, at the juncture between Upper and Lower Egypt. In the Old Kingdom, which followed the Early Dynastic Period, the kings were buried in the royal cemeteries at Sakkara and Giza just west of Memphis. The kings of the first two dynasties, however, chose to be buried at Abydos in Upper Egypt. These kings may have come from Abydos, or they may have chosen this site for religious reasons, since Abydos had been a sacred place from pre-dynastic times.

Abydos was the cult center of Osiris, king of the underworld and god of the dead. Osiris had ruled over Egypt in the mythological past before man, but when he was killed by his evil brother, Seth,

Osiris' son Horus then became ruler of the living and his deceased father ruled the realm of the dead. Thereafter each king of Egypt was equated with the god Horus when he was alive and the god Osiris when he died. Thus, each dead king became Osiris, and it was fitting that he be buried at Abydos.

Although larger and more elaborate, these early royal tombs took the same form as those of the king's officials and courtiers. The superstructure, or the part above ground marking the burial, was a mud-brick *mastaba*. Mastaba means "bench" in Arabic, and the tombs are so called because their rectangular shape resembles a large bench. A vertical shaft (later, slanting corridors were built instead) led to the burial chamber below the solid mastaba.

With the Third Dynasty, Egypt entered the Old Kingdom or Pyramid Age, composed of Dynasties Three to Six. Under King Zoser of the Third Dynasty, the first pyramid, the Step Pyramid of Sakkara, was built. The stepped pyramid shape developed from additions made to a central mastaba until there were six steps up each side. Not only was the Step Pyramid the first pyramid, but it also marked the first time the ancient Egyptians built with stone. The pyramid and the large complex around it were built entirely of small, brick-size limestone blocks, for the Egyptians were not yet used to working with stone. Their techniques developed quickly, however, and within a few generations Egyptian workmen built the Great Pyramid at Giza, in

which there are single blocks weighing as much as fifteen tons.

Pyramids built later than the Step Pyramid at Sakkara were "true" pyramids with smooth, cased sides. The shape of the pyramid reflects not only architectural but also religious development. Whereas the Step Pyramid served as a staircase by which the king could ascend to the stars, the newer pyramid became a sun-ray ramp for the king's ascension, and the religious emphasis shifted from a stellar to a solar orientation. The importance of the sun cult continued to grow throughout the Old Kingdom, and much later, in the Amarna Period of the New Kingdom, the sun cult even dominated for a short time.

By the end of the Fifth Dynasty, texts were inscribed on the chamber walls inside the pyramids. The spells given in these pyramid texts were to insure the resurrection of the dead king and his safe passage into the afterlife.

The Old Kingdom was a stable, peaceful period of Egyptian history. As the incarnation of the falcon god Horus, son of Osiris, the king ruled a bureaucratic hierarchy headed by himself and the vizier with unquestioned authority. In the beginning the vizier was always the king's son, thus assuring his loyalty to the throne. The country was divided into a series of governmental districts, *sepat*, which we call "nomes," each headed by a nomarch, a kind of provincial governor. By the end of the Old Kingdom these provincial nomarchs, particularly in Upper Egypt, grew extremely powerful.

Except for a few forays against nomads in the eastern Delta, there were no serious armed conflicts during the Old Kingdom. In fact, there is no evidence that there was even a standing army. Nevertheless, Egypt traded actively with neighboring countries, sending expeditions to Lebanon for cedar, to the Sinai for turquoise, to Somalia for incense, and south into the Sudan for exotic African goods.

Although the downfall of the Old Kingdom is often attributed to the disintegration of central control during the long, ninety-four-year reign of Pepy II at the end of the Sixth Dynasty, it was in fact brought about by natural causes. The so-called "Neolithic wet phase" came to an end, and the climate became much drier, rainfall ceased, and Nile levels lowered. The savannah plateaus on each side of the river valley became the deserts we know in Egypt today. Wildlife disappeared or moved farther south, and plant life died. Tomb inscriptions during this time speak of drought and famine. When the local nomarchs took control, trying to feed their people and protect their nomes, civil war broke out. This period of anarchy, called the First Intermediate Period, lasted about one hundred years.

Finally, a line of powerful rulers emerged from Thebes, and King Nebhepetre Mentuhotep of the Eleventh Dynasty reunified Egypt. His reign began the period referred to as the Middle Kingdom, once again a time of unification and centralized government.

The Middle Kingdom was composed mostly of kings from the Twelfth Dynasty, beginning with Amenemhet I, a vizier who usurped the throne. He was later assassi-

nated, the only Egyptian king to suffer that fate. The throne remained in his family's hands, however, since he insured his son's succession through coregency, a system of appointing an heir to rule jointly with the elder king. In this way, when the father died, the son was already functioning as king and there was no break in royal control.

The kings of the Twelfth Dynasty moved their residence away from Memphis slightly south to a place they called *Itja-tawy*, "Seizer of the Two Lands." The new capital was probably picked for strategic reasons, since it was located almost in the middle of the country. This important site has never yet been found.

In the Twelfth Dynasty the kings launched a series of military attacks against Nubia until they had subdued and colonized that region south of the Egyptian border. From the Egyptian border at the First Cataract of the Nile south to the Second Cataract, Egypt held Nubia with a chain of enormous mud-brick fortresses. Important to Egypt not only for its trade in African goods and its gold mines, Nubia also secured Egypt's southern border.

Later in the Twelfth Dynasty, Sesostris III completely restructured the central government, undermining the power of the local nomarchs and diminishing any threat to royal power. His successor on the throne, Amenemhet III, reclaimed vast tracts of land in the area of Fayum and increased Egypt's agricultural prosperity.

The Thirteenth Dynasty was a mere shadow of the Twelfth. Its rulers were a series of short-term, ineffectual kings who relied heavily on their viziers' power. Throughout this time, numbers of Asiatic nomads infiltrated the eastern Delta through the Sinai. Eventually the Hyksos, a western Semitic people, took the Delta by force and established their own capital at Avaris, from which they ruled Lower Egypt. Their rule was at least nominally accepted in other parts of Egypt as well. These pharaohs called themselves kings of Egypt and copied Egyptian traditions, choosing Seth, the brother of Osiris, for their god. Six of these Hyksos kings are known, and they form the Fifteenth Dynasty of Egypt.

It was not until the end of the Seventeenth Dynasty, under King Kamose, that the Egyptians attempted to rid their land of these foreign rulers. Complaining of having to share Egypt "with an Asiatic in the north and a Nubian in the south," Kamose managed to defeat the Egyptians loyal to the Hyksos king. Although he launched an attack upon the city of Avaris, he was not successful in driving the Hyksos from Egypt. This was to be accomplished by his brother, King Ahmose, the first king of the Eighteenth Dynasty and first ruler of the New Kingdom.

King Ahmose, brother and successor to Kamose, was the first ruler of the Eighteenth Dynasty. By year eleven of his reign, he had attacked and plundered the Hyksos capital of Avaris in the Egyptian Delta and driven the Hyksos invaders from Egyptian soil. He pursued them across the Sinai to the Palestinian city of Sharuhen, where he besieged them for three years before sacking the city. Ahmose then turned his attention to Egypt's southern border, restoring complete control over the area of Lower Nubia that had been held by the kings of the Twelfth Dynasty. Ahmose reunified the country and extended the New Kingdom's dominion to Egypt's former limits.

Ahmose was followed on the throne by his son Amenophis. Relatively little is known of his reign except that he led at least one military campaign in Syro-Palestine and another in Nubia. Amenophis I laid the groundwork for the great Eighteenth Dynasty when he justified his military actions by saying that he was "extending the boundaries of Egypt."

His only son died as an infant, so Amenophis I was succeeded by his brother-in-law Tuthmosis I. Since the legitimate right to the throne passed through the female line, a man of nonroyal blood could claim the throne through marriage to a king's daughter or sister. Although Tuthmosis I had a short reign of nine years, he was very active militarily. In Asia, or Syro-Palestine, he campaigned as far eastward as the Euphrates River. In the Sudan he raided as far south as the Fourth Cataract, probably destroying the Kushite city of Kerma above the Third Cataract in the process. The king of Kerma had controlled Lower Nubia following the withdrawal of Egyptian power at the end of the Middle Kingdom and had established commercial and diplomatic relations with the Hyksos in the Delta during the Second Intermediate Period.

Tuthmosis I boasts of his military accomplishments: "I made the boundaries of Egypt as far as that which the sun encircles. . . . I made Egypt the superior of every land." The first king to have his tomb cut in the Valley of the Kings, Tuthmosis I also began an extensive building program at the Temple of Amun at Karnak, adding two pylons and two obelisks.

His son Tuthmosis II, who was married to his own half sister, Queen Hatshepsut, followed him on the throne. Although he ruled for eighteen years, Tuthmosis II's mummy indicates he was a sickly individual and was perhaps even bedridden for much of his life. He named Tuthmosis III, a son by one of his minor wives, to succeed him.

Tuthmosis III was still a child, and power was actually in the hands of Queen Hatshepsut, who served as his regent. For at least two years Queen Hatshepsut was content with this position, but then she had herself crowned pharaoh. In her coronation text she implies that the god Amun had intervened to have her crowned because he was displeased by the kingship of Tuthmosis III. Although Queen Hatshepsut is best known for the obelisks she set up at the Karnak Temple and her terraced funerary temple at Deir el-Bahari at Thebes, her reign was not just one of beautification projects. Under her rule there were at least four military campaigns into Syro-Palestine and Nubia, one of which she seems to have personally led. The others she relegated to Tuthmosis III, for she had him trained to conduct military matters while she controlled internal affairs.

Queen Hatshepsut died, apparently of natural causes, in regnal year twenty-two, leaving Tuthmosis III as sole ruler. He began his reign by leading a campaign into Syro-Palestine, the first of sixteen in the space of twenty years. All the rulers and cities of Syro-Palestine became his vassals. The Annals of Tuthmosis III carved in the Temple of Karnak describe these campaigns and also list all the booty he brought back to the coffers of Amun, the god of the temple. Tuthmosis III expanded the Egyptian empire and brought great prosperity to his land.

Tuthmosis III was succeeded by his son Amenophis II, who is portrayed in ancient sources as an outstanding athlete, and he was succeeded in turn by his son Tuthmosis IV. Both these later kings struggled against the powerful Mesopotamian state of Mitanni over northern Syria, the northern border of Egypt's empire. After both Amenophis II and Tuthmosis IV campaigned in the region, diplomatic peace was achieved when Tuthmosis IV married the daughter of the king of Mitanni. This kind of marriage diplomacy continued in the reign of his son and successor, Amenophis III.

When Amenophis III took the throne, he ruled over a peaceful empire stretching from the Fourth Cataract in the Sudan to the Euphrates River in Mesopotamia. Diplomacy had replaced warfare, and it was a time of prosperity at home and abroad. Egypt's wealth was based not only on its empire, but also on the gold she possessed—gold eagerly sought by the other rulers of the ancient Near East. International correspondence (preserved in part in the Amarna Letters) and trade were carried on regularly between Egypt and the other major powers of the Near East.

During his first ten years as king, Amenophis III was an active sportsman, spending much of his time hunting wild cattle and lions. In the remaining thirty-eight years of his reign, however, he contracted many marriages with foreign princesses and conducted a large-scale building program. He married the sister or daughter or both of almost every ruler in the Near East, particularly those of

the Mitanni and Babylon. Amenophis III built the Luxor Temple (to which Ramses II added a court and pylon) and a massive funerary temple on the West Bank at Thebes. The temple is gone, but the enormous statues known today as the Colossi of Memnon still mark its entrance.

Amenophis III is perhaps most famous for being the father of Amenophis IV, who launched the Amarna Age. By the fifth year of his reign, Amenophis IV had changed his name, closed the Amun temple at Karnak, and moved to his new capital at Tell el-Amarna in Middle Egypt. All these radical changes were due to Amenophis' worship of the sun disc, the Aten. The sun and the cult of the sun had always been important in Egypt, but Amenophis introduced something new. He worshipped the actual disc of the sun, a thing, an idol. Egyptian gods had always appeared in human or animal form or a combination of the two, but the Aten was simply the sun's disc, always shown with rays streaming from it.

Amenophis proclaimed that this disc was the only god to be worshipped in Egypt. He renamed himself Akhenaten, "One Who Is Useful to the Sun Disc," and hid himself away in his new capital, Akhet-aten, "The Horizon of the Sun Disc." Nevertheless, except for Thebes (where Akhenaten built eight structures for the Aten), Tell el-Amarna (which was the new

capital and cult center), and Heliopolis (the cult center of the sun god Re), the new religion seems not to have affected a large part of Egypt. The worship of Aten was almost the private affair of the king and royal family.

Perhaps the greatest impact the Amarna Age had on Egyptian traditions was in the realm of art. Akhenaten made no attempt to hide physical faults and have himself portrayed in the traditional idealistic style. Instead, artistic representations of him show an odd-looking man with a long horsey face, sagging stomach, and fat thighs. The king's wife and daughters were likewise portrayed with these physical characteristics; thus the royal physique became the style for "the new art."

Rather than allowing himself to be portrayed only in cult and state scenes, Akhenaten had himself depicted as an affectionate family man, in the company of his wife and children. Certain mannerisms characteristic of the relaxed art style of the Amarna Age, such as the ribbon wafting behind the king's war helmet, never disappear from later Egyptian art.

Perhaps what most affected Egypt after the Amarna Age, however, was the tremendous backlash against it. It was still in the period of reaction to the reign of Akhenaten that the family of Ramses II took power and molded its rule of Egypt.

Tutankhaten was raised at the new capital of Akhet-aten, and (after possibly one short intervening reign), he followed Akhenaten to the throne. By the third year of his reign, the young king had changed his name to Tutankhamun ("Living Image of Amun"), moved back to the traditional capital at Memphis, and reopened the cult of Amun at Thebes. His reign was short, and it was followed by the even shorter four-year reign of the elderly army officer Ay.

Following Ay, Tutankhamun's general Horemheb took control, battling for what had been lost in Egypt's Asian empire and restoring order at home. Akhenaten had so ignored internal affairs while basking in the rays of his disc that government had come to a virtual standstill. An indication of how far things had gone awry is the strong edict Horemheb issued against corrupt officials—he even imposed the death penalty on any judge found taking a bribe.

As pharaoh, Horemheb was ideal. His only problem was that he produced no heir to the throne. He therefore chose his vizier, Pramses, to follow him. Shortening his name to Ramses, the grandfather of Ramses II took the throne as the first king of the Nineteenth Dynasty.

Ramses I begins what is called the Ramesside Period, so called because almost every one of the period's kings carried the name Ramses. This first Ramses descended from a line of military officers from Lower Egypt. He must have already been an older man when he succeeded Horemheb, for surviving records indicate a two-year reign at most. He was in turn followed by his son Seti I, "Man of Seth," probably so named because the family came from near the Hyksos city Avaris, where the god Seth was worshipped.

Seti I proclaimed himself "Bringer of the Renaissance" and set about restoring the glories of the Egyptian empire. He began a series of military campaigns in Syro-Palestine and Nubia, as well as an extensive building program. He defeated Libyans entering Egyptian territory from the west, but he failed to stop their infiltration completely. (Eventually, with the downfall of the New Kingdom, Libyan dynasties took over and ruled in Egypt during the Third Intermediate Period.) Seti also fought in Syria against the encroaching power of the Hittites, whose mighty empire centered in the Anatolian highlands of modern-day Turkey.

Seti I's building program was designed to reestablish the traditional cults of Egypt. At Abydos, the most sacred place in Egypt since prehistoric times, he built an unusually shaped and beautifully decorated temple with seven sacred shrines joining the seven main religious cults of Egypt. The gods worshipped there were King Seti himself, Ptah, Re-Horachty, Amun-Re, Osiris, Isis, and Horus.

It is in this temple that the famous Abydos King List is located. Offerings were made to this list of the past kings of Egypt as part of the daily cult ritual called "The Ritual of the Ancestors." Ramses II, who would complete the decoration of the temple, is shown as a young crown prince standing before the king list "reciting praises" from a papyrus roll.

Seti I also completed the Hypostyle Hall at Karnak, which his father, Ramses I, had begun. This vast forest of columns forms the largest internal hall of any Egyptian temple. Seti's reliefs decorate its northern half and those of Ramses II its southern half. The decoration scheme is the same on both sides: cult and offering scenes are on the inside walls, and battle scenes are on the outside walls.

The last impressive monument left by Seti I is his tomb in the Valley of the Kings. Descending more than three hundred feet into solid rock, it is the longest tomb in the valley.

The young prince Ramses was Seti's eldest son by his chief queen Tuya. During the reign of his father, Ramses took an ever-increasing role in royal affairs, so by the time he became king, he had acquired considerable practical experience. Ramses was especially well trained for conducting war. The young prince's first experience on the battlefield came when he accompanied his father, Seti, in his regnal year five campaign against the Libyans. The next year he went with his father on a campaign in Syria.

During the second half of Seti's reign, Ramses began to take part in his father's building projects. He completed Seti's temple at Abydos and built one for himself nearby. Later he completed the decoration in the south half of the Hypostyle Hall at Karnak and that of his father's funerary temple on the other side of the river at Qurna.

By the end of his father's sixteen-year reign, Ramses was not only a builder and administrator, but a skilled warrior as well. He took the throne proclaiming his royal titles as *Horus, Strong Bull, Beloved of Ma'at; The Two Goddesses, Protector of Egypt, Subduer of Foreign Lands; Horus of Gold, Rich in Years, Great of Victories; King of Upper and Lower Egypt, The Truth of Re Is Strong;* and *Son of Re, Ramses II, Beloved of Amun.*

The King as Warrior

In year five of his own reign, Ramses II led his army to the city of Kadesh on the Orontes River. Here he hoped to defeat the Hittites and force them to withdraw from northern Syria. The events of the Battle of Kadesh are preserved for us in detail in the official report of the battle, called The Bulletin, and the narrative account, called The Poem. Along with these written accounts we have a pictorial record. Ramses not only had the battle depicted on the inside northern wall of the temple at Abu Simbel, but on the first pylon of the Luxor Temple and the second pylon of the Ramesseum as well.

The army left Egypt and began the march through the Gaza Strip, Canaan, and southern Syria. The pharaoh's four divisions of soldiers were each named after an Egyptian god. Ramses himself led the division of Amun, which was followed by those of Re, Ptah, and Seth. A separate support force went up the coast and was to cut east, meeting Ramses at Kadesh.

One month after leaving Egypt, the king and his army arrived a few miles outside Kadesh. Leaving the other three divisions spread out behind, the king and the Amun Division hurriedly set out for the city. On the way, two local tribesmen in league with the Hittites approached the king. They told him that the Hittite king, Muwatallis, was afraid of the pharaoh's advance and had retreated far to the north. Pleased with this news, Ramses and his division began to set up camp to the west of Kadesh.

At this point two Hittite spies were captured, and they admitted upon being beaten that the Hittite king and a large army were behind Kadesh on the east side. In the midst of Ramses II's hurried emergency meeting with his generals, the Hittites attacked.

Hittite chariots crossed the Orontes and smashed through the Re Division marching toward the Egyptian camp. Then the chariots swept into the Amun Division, panicking the pharaoh's troops. Ramses leapt into his chariot and practically held off the Hittites single-handedly. Fortunately, the Egyptian support troops from the coast arrived at this critical point. The Hittite troops were surrounded, and the Egyptians pushed them back across the river. At the river's edge Ramses called a halt in order to regroup. Before the end of the day they were joined by the divisions of Ptah and Seth.

The next day Ramses led the attack. Although the Hittites had lost almost all their chariots the day before, they had an army twice the size of the Egyptians'. The armies fought to a stalemate, and both sides withdrew. The Battle of Kadesh was over.

Ramses returned to Egypt in triumph, but he had not dislodged the Hittites from northern Syria. During the next five years he had to return to Syro-Palestine to put down three revolts against Egyptian rule.

Finally, in the twenty-first year of his reign, Ramses II and the

Hittite king Hattusilis III signed a peace treaty. Copies of the text of the treaty have been found in Egypt, as well as in the Hittite capital of Hattusas. The treaty was composed in three ancient languages: Egyptian, Hittite, and the international diplomatic language of the time, Akkadian. Its terms were basically those of nonaggression and mutual defense. With this treaty the Egyptian and Hittite power struggle came to an end. In fact, relations improved so much that by regnal year thirty-four Ramses II married the daughter of the Hittite king.

The King as Builder

More than any other pharaoh, Ramses II was a prodigious builder; and if he did not build a structure himself, he put his name on it. His most famous buildings are temples: the Ramesseum, the Luxor Temple, and the Abu Simbel temples in Nubia.

The Ramesseum is the funerary temple of Ramses II located on the West Bank of Thebes. Each royal tomb in the Valley of the Kings required a funerary, or mortuary, temple in which the rituals of the king's cult could be performed. These temples were built along the edge of the valley cultivation in front of the Theban cliffs.

Construction of both the funerary temple and the royal tomb began when the king was crowned. Although the temple was to serve the cult of the king in perpetuity, it began functioning as soon as the building was completed. In fact, a palace where Ramses stayed when visiting Thebes was built off the side of the temple's first court.

Ancient Egyptians named their buildings, and the funerary temple of Ramses II was called "The House of Millions of Years of Ramses II in the Estate of Amun." Although the temple was built to serve the royal cult, its main shrine was built to honor the god Amun, for at Thebes the cults of the god and the king were fused. The divine image of Amun of Karnak would also visit each funerary temple once a year during the "Beautiful Festival of the Valley."

On the other side of the river, or the East Bank of Thebes, Ramses II added a court, front pylon, and obelisks to the Temple of Luxor. This temple, built earlier by Amenophis III, served as a subsidiary to the main Amun temple at Karnak. Once each year, at the beginning of the Egyptian New Year, the images of Amun and his consort, Mut, would be transported from their own respective temples at Karnak and south Karnak to the Luxor Temple for a honeymoon stay. The New Year, which occurred in mid-summer, was heralded by the rising of the Dog Star, Sirius, and coincided with the rising of the Nile. At this time the king traveled to Thebes from his residence in the

north. While he was in Upper Egypt for the Amun Festival, officials were promoted and rewarded, and the public ate and drank at the king's expense.

Ramses' construction of the Luxor Temple was finished in the third year of his reign. The decoration, however, took somewhat longer. A depiction of the Battle of Kadesh was added to the front of the pylon some time after regnal year five.

Because their rescue from the rising waters of Lake Nasser in the 1960s received such worldwide publicity, the two Abu Simbel temples are undoubtedly the best known of all Ramses II's monuments. The main temple was dedicated to Ramses himself, along with the gods Re-Horachty, Amun, and Ptah. The smaller temple was dedicated to the goddess Hathor and the chief queen Nefertari. Although the size and complexity of the two temples differ (the Ramses temple is almost exactly twice the size of the queen's temple), the basic plan of each is the same: carved façade, pillared interior hall, and shrine at the rear.

Four seated colossal statues of Ramses II, each sixty-five feet high, form the façade of the main temple. Inside the main hall Osiride, or mummiform, figures of the king are carved on the pillars. On its north interior wall is the most complete pictorial version of the Battle of Kadesh. Each event of the battle is depicted, spread out in a great panorama over the entire wall. In the back shrine, carved some 160 feet into the mountain, sit the four deity figures of the temple. On the leftmost is Ptah, then Amun, the king, and Re-Horachty. The axis of the temple is so aligned that two times during the year the rays of the sun penetrate to illuminate three of these figures. The sun shines directly on the form of Ramses II. The figure of Ptah, however, whose cult has no solar connections, is always left in the dark.

The façade of the smaller temple is the same on each side of the doorway: two striding figures of Ramses flank a standing figure of Queen Nefertari. Accompanying each of the large figures are much smaller ones representing the royal children. Inside, instead of pillars featuring statues of the king, are Hathor-headed columns. The cult figure at the back of the shrine, however, is once again Ramses, this time protected by the cow of Hathor.

Ramses II did indeed build more than any other pharaoh, but he sacrificed quality for quantity. This is most evident at the Abydos Temple he completed for his father. The stone carver in Seti's reign carved in raised relief, cutting back around the figures and hieroglyphs and leaving them raised from the surface of the wall. The workmen under Ramses II simply cut the decoration into the stone, using incised or sunken technique. This method is much faster than raised relief and requires less skill. The different parts of the temple belonging to Seti I and Ramses II are obvious: where raised relief decoration stops, sunken relief begins.

The Royal Family

In an inscription at Abydos Ramses II described how he was crowned heir apparent by his father, Seti I. Seti also seems to have chosen his son's consorts at this time, for Ramses said: "He established me with a female household, a king's harem similar to the beauties of the palace. He picked wives for me."

Ramses' chief and favorite queen was Nefertari. She appears with the king on his monuments from the first year of his reign. Ramses carved the smaller of the two temples at Abu Simbel in her honor and had what is considered to be the most beautiful of the queens' tombs cut for her in the Valley of the Queens. Nefertari's two main titles as queen are recorded in this tomb: "King's Great Wife" and "Mistress of the Two Lands." The title "King's Great Wife" reflects her importance over the other queens of the harem, as well as her position as mother of the royal heir. "Mistress of the Two Lands" parallels the king's "Lord of the Two Lands" and indicates the queen was in a position of some authority.

In her tomb, as well as on the façade of her temple at Abu Simbel, the queen is depicted wearing a crown with sun disc, cow horns, and two tall ostrich plumes. The disc and horns are those of the cow goddess Hathor, consort to the falcon god Horus. Because the king was "Horus, on the Throne of the Living," Nefertari as his wife assumed Hathor's symbols. Beginning with the New Kingdom, the king was revered as the physical son of the god Amun, who was to have appeared and impregnated the chief queen. Nefertari wore feathers identical to those on the god's crown to symbolize that she was the wife of Amun.

Nefertari's eldest son, Amun-her-khepeshef, appointed heir apparent by Ramses, was to be the first of many sons who predeceased their long-lived father. He died as a boy and was buried in a tomb near his mother's in the Valley of the Queens.

The children of Ramses' second chief queen, Ist-nofret, came into prominence after Nefertari's had died. One son, Merneptah, ultimately succeeded his father to the throne. Another, Khaemwaset, died before his father but became famous in his own right. During forty years' service in the priesthood of the god Ptah, he established the Serapeum, the underground burial gallery for the sacred Apis bulls at Sakkara, and restored a number of Old Kingdom monuments in the royal cemeteries at Giza and Sakkara. Khaemwaset was venerated as a sage by later generations and was posed as the magician hero in a series of Graeco-Roman stories.

These queens and princes are the most prominent of Ramses II's family. Numerous other wives included two Hittite princesses; his own daughter by Queen Ist-nofret, Bint-Anath; and his daughter by Queen Nefertari, Meryet-amun. His children numbered more than one hundred.

The King's Death

Ramses II died in the second month of his sixty-seventh year of reign, probably at the age of ninety-two. His death occurred in the summer of 1213 or 1224 B.C., depending on which chronology of ancient Egypt is followed. While his son and successor, Merneptah, was being crowned, the body of Ramses was prepared for burial.

In accordance with the ancient Egyptian tradition of mummification, Ramses II's inner organs were removed, mummified separately, and placed in four containers called canopic jars. The body itself was dried with natron and salt and treated with spices, resins, and oils. This part of the process took seventy days. Then the body was packed with stuffing to look lifelike and wrapped in linen. Finally, the body was enclosed in a series of nested coffins (probably made of gold) and conveyed on a royal barge to Thebes for burial.

Ramses II's tomb (Tomb Seven) in the Valley of the Kings lies near the modern entrance to the east valley. A corridor divided into seven successive halls descends on a northwest line in the tomb and then makes a right angle turn toward the northeast into the pillared burial chamber. Seven smaller rooms for storing funerary objects and equipment lead from the chamber.

Special funerary texts, all designed to assure the king's resurrection in the afterlife, decorate the walls of the tomb. The first part of the descending corridor is carved with the "Litany of Re," a text that gives the numerous names and praises of the sun god. A text called the *Amduat*, the "Book of What Is in the Underworld," follows. The underworld is divided into twelve regions, each of which corresponds to one of the hours of night. The king had to pass safely through these hours before his rebirth in the morning.

At the very end of this descending corridor, before it turns in the direction of the burial chamber, is the text of the "Ritual of the Opening of the Mouth." This ritual entailed touching particular parts of the body with special implements so that each body part (eyes, ears, nose, mouth, etc.) could function again in the afterlife.

The burial chamber itself was called the "House of Gold," perhaps referring to the golden coffins and shrines in which the body of the king lay. This chamber was decorated with parts of the *Amduat* text, as well as parts of the "Book of the Gates." Very similar to the *Amduat*, the "Book of the Gates" described the underworld as a series of compartments, each with a guardian at its gate. As with the twelve regions of the night, the king had to pass through each gate to reach the afterlife.

In modern times the tomb of Ramses II was found empty and plundered. The mummy, however, was preserved and is now in the Cairo Museum. During the chaos that prevailed in Thebes at the end of the Twentieth Dynasty, Ramses' tomb must have been disturbed, for the High Priest of Amun Herihor had it rewrapped.

In the Twenty-first Dynasty, the mummies of Ramses II and his father, Seti I, along with a number of other royal mummies, were removed from their tombs and reburied in the cliffs at Deir el-Bahari. There the mummies were discovered by the Department of Antiquities in 1881 and removed to Cairo.

The mummy of Ramses II shows that he was 1.73 meters (5 feet 6.5 inches) tall. He was bald on the top of his head and had severe dental problems, including both extreme wear and periodontal disease. He also had extensive arteriosclerosis, to be expected of an elderly person.

Ramses II had such a lengthy reign that Merneptah, his thirteenth son, was already more than fifty years old when he assumed the throne. Five years later Merneptah fought a coalition of Libyan tribes in the Western Desert. The king describes the battle on a stela, on which he not only recounts the victory over the Libyans, but near the end he also states that other countries and peoples have been conquered or plundered, including Israel. This stela is often called "The Israel Stela," since it contains the first mention of the word Israel in an ancient Egyptian text. As Merneptah lists the peoples, countries, and cities he has vanquished, he says: "Israel is wasted, bare of seed." Most scholars assume that at this point the Israelites had settled as a tribe in Palestine, following forty years of wandering in the wilderness. Therefore the Exodus must have taken place some time during the reign of Ramses II.

From the end of Merneptah's reign to the end of the Nineteenth Dynasty is a period of approximately twenty-three years. During this time three kings and one queen ruled, but their reigns were extremely short, and there are even questions about the exact order in which they ruled.

The Twentieth Dynasty began with the two-year reign of Setnakht, followed by that of Ramses III, the dynasty's most famous king. Ramses III reigned for thirty-two years, and the events

of his reign are well known to us both from the inscriptions at his funerary temple at Medinet Habu and numerous papyri. He fought three major wars, the most important of which took place in the eighth year of his reign. Ramses III's army held off an invasion of Egypt by the Sea People, a confederation of nomadic people who had swept down through the Levant destroying everything in their path. Ramses III describes slaughtering them "like birds, ensnared in the net," when they entered the branches of the Nile flowing into the Egyptian Delta.

Besides invasions, internal problems plagued Ramses III as well. In the twenty-ninth year of his reign, the workmen at Deir el-Medina went on strike because the government was behind in paying their wages. This is the first known strike in ancient Egypt. In addition, there was a harem conspiracy against Ramses III in which a minor queen attempted to have him killed so that her son could take the throne. The proceedings of the trial and the punishment of the guilty are preserved for us in the "Juridical Papyrus" in the Turin Museum.

From the end of Ramses III's reign to the end of the Twentieth Dynasty is a period of about one hundred thirteen years. During this time the pharaohs Ramses IV to Ramses XI reigned. These kings

were almost all sons of Ramses III, so the royal succession was often from brother to brother rather than from father to son.

From the reign of Ramses IX we have a series of papyri known as "The Tomb Robbery Papyri" that document an investigation into the robbing of royal tombs on the West Bank at Thebes. Suspects confessed and were punished, but these arrests, trials, and punishments did not end the problem. Plundering the tombs began again in the reign of Ramses XI, perhaps as part of a civil war that seems to have broken out in the Theban area. This unrest was compounded by Libyans raiding western Thebes from the desert. The workmen at Deir el-Medina, no longer safe in their secluded village, deserted it and moved inside the walls of the mortuary temple of Ramses III nearby at Medinet Habu.

In the nineteenth year of Ramses XI's reign, his general Herihor became high priest of Amun and declared a "Renaissance." Based at Thebes, Herihor controlled Upper Egypt while Ramses XI remained in his palace in the Delta. This power split was to continue through the

Third Intermediate Period, which began with the death of Ramses XI and the end of the Twentieth Dynasty.

During the Third Intermediate Period, extending from Dynasties Twenty-one to Twenty-five, the king ruled Lower Egypt while the high priest of Amun ruled Upper Egypt. The infiltration of Libyans from the west continued unabated, and in the Twenty-first Dynasty the western Delta was controlled by Libyan chieftains. By the Twenty-second Dynasty not only had the Libyans taken control of the Delta, but Libyans ruled during the rest of the Third Intermediate Period.

The Twenty-first Dynasty ruled from the city of Tanis in the eastern Delta. Royal burials no longer took place in the Valley of the Kings at Thebes; instead, mummies were buried within the enclosure of the Amun Temple at Tanis. It was here that the tomb and treasure of Psusennes I was discovered.

In Thebes, the mummies of earlier pharaohs whose graves had been plundered were placed in common burial areas, which were more easily guarded than numerous separate tombs. The mummy of Ramses II was among those reburied.

By 715 B.C. three Libyan dynasties, Dynasties Twenty-two, Twenty-three, and Twenty-four, were ruling simultaneously from cities in the Delta. They seem to have made some threat against Thebes, for Piye, a Kushite ruler from the Sudan, came north to Egypt to protect the cult of Amun at Thebes. He defeated the Libyans and their supporters and began the Twenty-fifth Dynasty, the Kushite Dynasty.

The Kushite kings ruled in Egypt but returned to their homeland of Napata, just below the Fourth Cataract in the Sudan, to be buried. Here they built small pyramids imitating those in Egypt. During the reign of the fourth king, Taharqa, the conflict between Egypt and the Assyrians began. In 664–663 B.C. the Assyrians were successful in invading Egypt as far as Thebes, where they sacked the city. A thousand years of treasure was plundered and carried away from the Temple of Amun.

This disaster ended Kushite rule. The Saite or Twenty-sixth Dynasty, based at the city of Sais in the Delta, was then set up as vassal to the Assyrian Empire. With this dynasty began the so-called Late Period, composed of Dynasties Twenty-six to Thirty-one. The Late Period was basically one of foreign domination over Egypt, broken by short spells of independent Egyptian rule. During the longest of these dynasties, the Twenty-seventh, Persian kings ruled Egypt as part of the Persian Empire.

In 332 B.C. Alexander the Great defeated the Persian Empire and, along with its other territories, took possession of Egypt. With the death of Alexander in 323 B.C., pharaonic history came to an end. Afterward, Alexander's general Ptolemy I began a period of Greek rule in Egypt that lasted until 30 B.C., when the Romans conquered Egypt and made it part of the Roman Empire.

DATE	HISTORICAL PERIOD	SIGNIFICANT EVENTS/ACHIEVEMENTS
Before 4000 B.C.	Paleolithic man	
4000 B.C. to 3100 B.C.	Neolithic man, predynastic cultures	
3100 B.C.	Unification of Egypt	*Writing appears*
3100 B.C. to 2700 B.C.	Early Dynastic Period, Dynasties 1–2	*Narmer unites Egypt, Memphis founded*
2700 B.C. to 2200 B.C.	Old Kingdom, Dynasties 3–6	*"Pyramid Age"*
2200 B.C. to 2040 B.C.	First Intermediate Period, Dynasties 7–10, Early Dynasty 11	*Climate change, civil war, reunited by Mentuhotep*
2040 B.C. to 1715 B.C.	Middle Kingdom, Late Dynasty 11, Dynasty 12, Early Dynasty 13	*Capital at Itja-tawy, Lower Nubia colonized, central government restructured*
1715 B.C. to 1552 B.C.	Second Intermediate Period, Dynasties 13–17	*Hyksos invasion, Dynasty 15—Hyksos rulers, Thebans begin struggle for independence*
1552 B.C. to 1069 B.C.	New Kingdom, Dynasties 18–20	*Ahmose drives out Hyksos, Tuthmose III enlarges Egyptian empire to its greatest extent, Amarna Age under Akhenaten, Dynasties 19–20—Ramesside Period, Reign of Ramses II (Dynasty 19, 1290–1224 B.C.)*
1069 B.C. to 650 B.C.	Third Intermediate Period, Dynasties 21–25	*Egypt divided, king in Delta—high priest of Amun in Upper Egypt, Libyans rule by Dynasty 22, Kushites reunite Egypt, Assyrian invasion*
650 B.C. to 323 B.C.	Late Period, Dynasties 26–31	*Egypt, vassal of Assyria, conquered by Persian Empire, taken by Alexander the Great (332 B.C.), death of Alexander (323 B.C.)*
323 B.C. to 30 B.C.	Ptolemaic or Greek Period	
30 B.C.	Egypt becomes part of the Roman Empire	
200 A.D. to 640 A.D.	Christian Egypt	
395 A.D. to 640 A.D.	Byzantine Period	
640 A.D.	Islamic conquest	

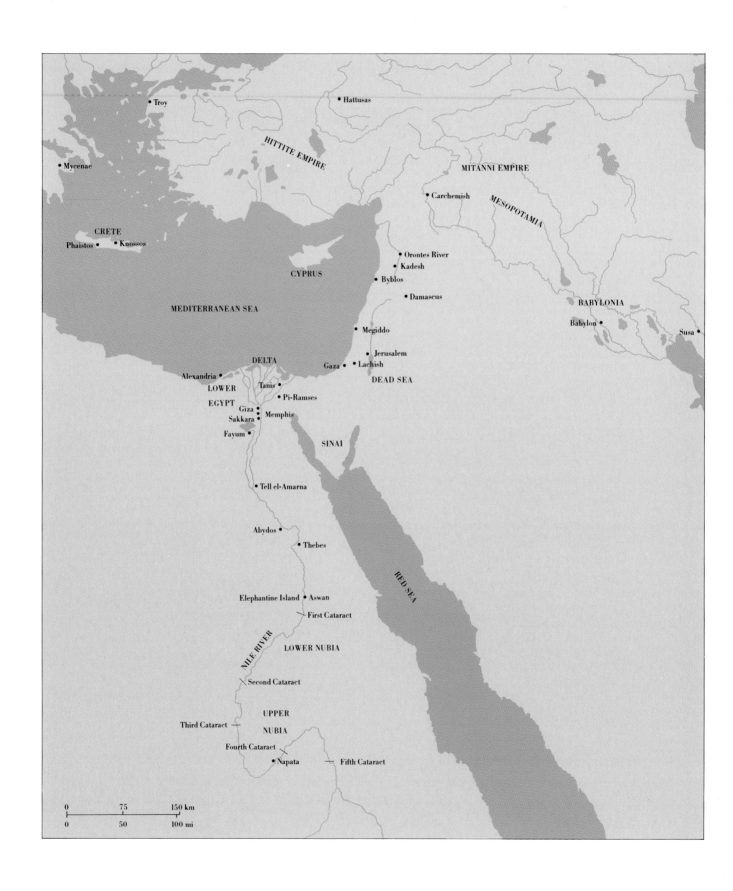

- Troy
- Hattusas
- Mycenae

HITTITE EMPIRE

MITANNI EMPIRE

- Carchemish

MESOPOTAMIA

CRETE

- Phaistos
- Knossos

CYPRUS

- Orontes River
- Kadesh
- Byblos

MEDITERRANEAN SEA

- Damascus

BABYLONIA

- Babylon

- Susa

- Megiddo

DELTA

- Jerusalem

- Alexandria

Gaza • Lachish

LOWER

- Tanis

DEAD SEA

EGYPT

- Pi-Ramses

Giza •

- Memphis

Sakkara •

Fayum •

SINAI

- Tell el-Amarna

Abydos •

- Thebes

RED SEA

Elephantine Island • Aswan

- First Cataract

NILE RIVER

LOWER NUBIA

- Second Cataract

UPPER

Third Cataract —

NUBIA

Fourth Cataract —

- Napata

— Fifth Cataract

| 0 | 75 | 150 km |
| 0 | 50 | 100 mi |

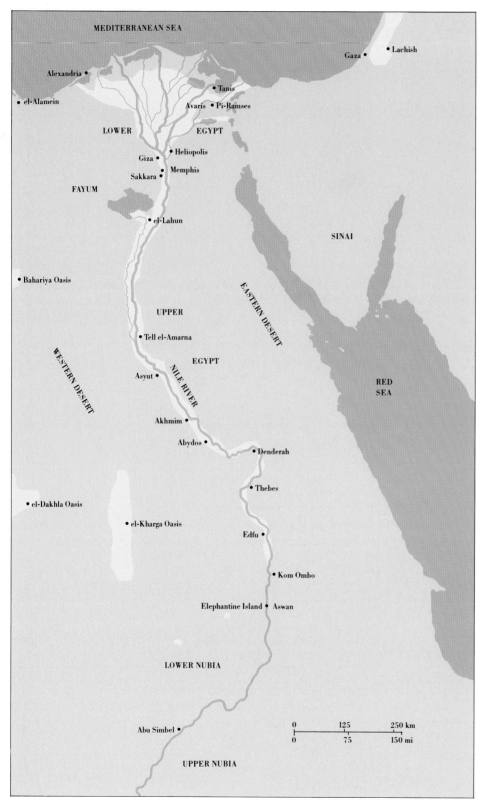

The major civilizations in existence at the time of Ramses II (Near Eastern Map) were the Minoan-Mycenaean world of Greece and the Greek islands, the Hittite Empire (modern-day Turkey), the Mitanni of northern Mesopotamia, and Babylonia in southern Mesopotamia. Most of the sites noted on the Egyptian Map were significant during the reign of Ramses II, though a few such as Alexandria and el-Alamein were named or founded at a later time.

The three drums of this redecorated column were found on the island of Elephantine in foundations dating to the time of the Roman emperor Trajan. Because a column of vertical inscription down one side carries his titulary, it is assumed the column was originally set up by the pharaoh Tuthmosis IV. Then, in the next dynasty, Ramses II had his figure and titles cut on another side of the column.

The figure of Ramses, cut in sunken relief, is preserved from the waist up. The king wears the blue war helmet with uraeus coiled on the front and two ribbons hanging down in back. Around his neck are two rows of gold beads. He holds three lotuses in his left hand and supports a more formal, standing bouquet with his right. At his waist the wide belt of his kilt is partially visible.

Above and to the left of Ramses are his prenomen and nomen, that is, his throne name and his birth name. A cartouche encloses each of the names. Above this the protective falcon god Horus spreads his wings over the king. In his claws is the *shen*-sign, the hieroglyphic word meaning "encircle," for Horus is encircling and protecting the king.

Traces of paint can still be seen in the pleats of the king's linen gown across his left shoulder. Blue paint remains on the lotus flowers, the king's helmet, and the wings of the falcon. Red paint still exists in some of the hieroglyphs and on the helmet's ribbons.

Cairo Museum entry no.: 41560.
Height: 1.62 m.
Provenance: Elephantine Island.
Date: New Kingdom, Dynasties 18 and 19.

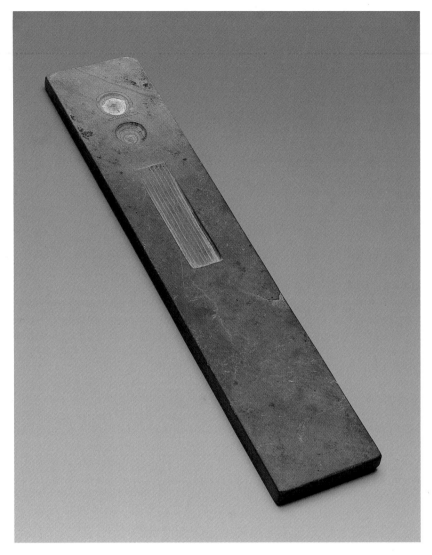

A palette was an indispensable item for the ancient Egyptian scribe. Generally made of wood so that it was portable, it carried the scribe's ink and pens. The ink, in two cakes, was set in circular depressions at the top of the palette. The scribe needed two colors, black for writing and red for headings and corrections. The black ink was made from carbon or soot, mixed with gum, and then dried in small cakes. The red ink was made in a similar fashion but from red ochre. The long, vertical body of the palette would have been hollowed out with a slot so that the reed pens could fit inside. The scribe would also carry a water pot in which to wet his writing pens.

Since this palette, found at Tell el-Ruba'a, is made of schist, and the slot for the pens has never been completed, it was meant to be placed in the tomb as a funerary offering. The Book of the Dead, a collection of spells recited to insure safe entry into the afterlife, has a spell to guarantee the deceased access to scribal equipment. In case the spell failed, this palette was provided so the scribe could draw upon the written secrets of Thoth, the god of writing.

Cairo Museum entry no.: SR305＝C. 69033.
Length: 32.3 cm. Width: 6 cm.
Provenance: Tell el-Ruba'a.
Date: Late Period.

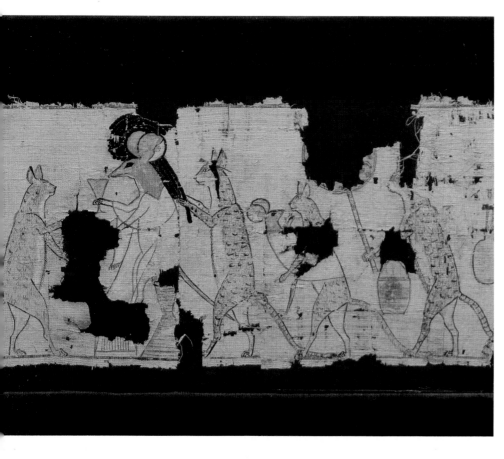

There are a number of papyri and ostraca (inscribed pottery fragments) from ancient Egypt that playfully depict animals in human situations or performing human tasks. In the drawing on this papyrus, not only are animals grooming, tending, and feeding other animals, but some perform tasks for animals upon which they would normally prey. Cats are serving mice, and foxes are feeding cattle.

At the left, a mouse in a long linen gown sits while one cat serves her wine in a chalice and another grooms her elegant wig. A third cat tends the mouse's baby while a fourth bears a fan and jug of liquid. On the right, facing in the other direction, one fox serves as water bearer while another pours water into a trough for a penned cow. A fragment at the far right of the papyrus shows another fox at work.

The outlines of the animals are drawn in black over lighter red lines. The mouse's gown and the pieces of equipment held by the cats and foxes were left in the initial red. The bodies of the cats and the foxes have been shaded in light brown and the details of the fur added in black. The mouse's wig is black and the cow's horns and trough are blue.

Cairo Museum entry no.: 31199.
Maximum height: 13 cm.
Total length: 55.5 cm.
Provenance: Purchased.
Date: New Kingdom, Dynasty 20 (?).

This grey granite statue depicts the high official Ramses-nakht seated as a scribe. He sits trancelike under the protection of the baboon of Thoth, god of writing, pondering the mystery of the great deity.

Ramses-nakht wears a typical Ramesside Period long linen gown with flaring sleeves. His garment has been pulled across the body in such a way that the lines of the abdomen underneath are shown. His somewhat flaccid physique indicates that he is an older man. His skirt, pulled tight across the knees, forms the surface on which he writes. He unrolls a papyrus scroll with one hand and writes with the other. The text on his lap gives his official titles.

The inscription on the base repeats Ramses-nakht's most prestigious title: "High Priest of Amun." By this time in Egyptian history, the high priest at Thebes was one of the most important officials in the country and virtual ruler of the Theban area.

This statue was discovered in the Karnak cachette, a group of statues and other pieces removed from the Karnak Temple in ancient times and found reburied in the Court of the Seventh Pylon of the Temple of Karnak. In the later New Kingdom this common form of seated scribe statue was often dedicated to the god Amun.

Cairo Museum entry no.: 36582.
Museum catalog no.: 42162.
Height: 75 cm. Width: 43 cm.
Depth: 39 cm.
Provenance: Thebes.
Date: New Kingdom, Dynasty 20.

A mullet, *Mugil cephalus*, one of the most common Nile fishes, is depicted on this glazed tile fragment. Made of a silica composition, such tiles were first molded by hand and dried. Then they were painted, glazed in different colors, and fired.

These tiles might have been set in the floors or along the dado, or bottom half, of a palace wall. The tiles used in the public portions of the palace, particularly in the throne and reception rooms, depicted bound captive figures or were decorated with the names and titles of the king. The tiles in the private rooms, on the other hand, featured more relaxed and natural scenes: gardens, lakes, and ponds, complete with fauna. Famous examples of such scenes were found in the royal quarters of the complex at Tell el-Amarna, and these Ramesside decorative tiles from the palace at Qantir reflect the same Amarna Age influence.

The mullet is also commonly shown in tomb scenes dealing with the catching and drying of fish and sometimes with the extraction of roe.

The water in which the fish is swimming is represented by zigzag lines in the background. Both an open and a closed lotus appear near the fish.

Cairo Museum entry no.: 89484.
Length: 17.2 cm. Width: 13.2 cm.
Provenance: Qantir.
Date: New Kingdom, Dynasty 19.

This tile fragment shows a Nile bulti, *Tilapia nilotica* (see also object 61), swimming in water represented by zigzag lines. In ancient times the name of this fish was *inet*, but it also came to be referred to as *wajd*, meaning "green" or "fresh." This fish became associated with the idea of fertility or rebirth, and it was often depicted with the lotus flower, which is also a symbol of rebirth. The fish and lotus shown together on this tile form a decorative motif, as well as a double guarantee of resurrection.

Cairo Museum entry no.: 89479.
Length: 31.5 cm. Width: 16 cm.
Provenance: Qantir.
Date: New Kingdom, Dynasty 19.

This large grey granite statue shows the young child Ramses II protected by the god Hauron, depicted as a falcon. When it was found, part of the falcon's face and head were broken away, but they have since been restored in limestone.

Hauron is a Syrian god whose cult was introduced into Egypt in the mid-Eighteenth Dynasty. At Tanis, where this statue was found, Hauron is depicted as the falcon god Horus, whereas at Giza he is associated with the Great Sphinx. King Amenhotep II built a shrine for Hauron near the Sphinx, and Tutankhamun and Ramses II later added to that shrine.

The young king is shown crouching between the legs of the falcon, his hair gathered in a lock that falls down the right side of his head and his finger to his mouth. Both characteristics are conventions representing a child. Ramses has a sun disc on his head and holds the Upper Egyptian *swt*-plant in his left hand. The disc, child, and plant are all hieroglyphic signs that form a rebus for the name Ramses: the disc is *Re*, the child *mes*, and the plant *su*.

There is a short inscription on each side of the base. The throne name of Ramses appears on the front, and his birth name is used on the other three sides. On each of the long sides of the base, after the king's name, Ramses is called "Beloved of Hauron."

Cairo Museum entry no.: 64735.
Height: 2.31 m. Base length: 1.3 m.
Base width: 64.5 cm.
Provenance: Tanis.
Date: New Kingdom, Dynasty 19.

This black granite statue depicts the high official Khay seated with his knees pulled up and his arms across them. This type of sculpture is referred to as a "block statue" because of its square, blocklike appearance. In the rectangle formed by Khay's body, the façade of a shrine has been cut. Inside, hand in hand, stand Amun-Re (with his tall, ostrich feather crown) and his consort, Mut. The inscriptions on the base below and the shrine above are divided exactly in half. Khay asks for life, prosperity, and health from Amun-Re on the left side and for long life from Mut on the right.

Three vertical lines of inscription on the back of the statue give Khay's titles, including "Hereditary Prince," "Count," "Dignitary," "Mayor of Thebes," "Vizier," and "Prophet of Ma'at."

Khay served as vizier of Upper Egypt during the middle years of Ramses II's reign. Among his other duties as vizier he was in charge of organizing the jubilee, or *heb-sed*, festival of the king. A stela of Khay at Gebel Silsileh south of Thebes explains how the king directed Khay to arrange his fifth jubilee in regnal year 42. The cartouches of Ramses II are carved on Khay's shoulders.

This statue was found in the cachette in the Temple of Karnak (see also objects 19 and 20).

Cairo Museum entry no.: 37406.
Museum catalog no.: 42165.
Height: 73 cm.
Provenance: Thebes.
Date: New Kingdom, Dynasty 19.

This fragmentary scene of dignitaries in procession is preserved on two blocks of sandstone from a nobleman's tomb on the West Bank of Thebes. One complete register and the bottom of another above it are visible. In both, lines of officials bowed in respect are proceeding to the right, undoubtedly toward the king. They are all barefoot and each wears a long linen gown.

The men with shaven heads wear long gowns that begin at chest level and are held up by two shoulder straps. This is the traditional dress of the vizier, the man second in charge under the king. Under Ramses II, as during the rest of the New Kingdom, there were two viziers, one of the north, or Lower Egypt, and one of the south, or Upper Egypt. One of these figures in the center holds a scepter with the hieroglyphic for *west* or *right*. This marks him as an official placed on the right side of the king. He also holds the crook and the royal scarf. Some of the other dignitaries hold a papyrus scroll or long cane.

Behind the row of dignitaries is a table piled with objects, including gold collars, which are probably to be conferred on these men by the king. In the fragmentary band of inscription just below this scene, the word *djadjat*, "magistrates," appears, referring to the men pictured in procession.

Cairo Museum entry no.: 14–6–24–20.
Special register no.: 11775.
Minimum height: 1.02 m.
Maximum width: 1.17 m.
Provenance: Thebes.
Date: New Kingdom, Dynasty 19.

These faience pieces inlaid with colored paste once formed a floral frieze on a Ramesside palace wall in the Delta. The frieze is composed of lotus blossoms separated by triangular-shaped pieces. The triangles have a golden background with either a bunch of grapes or a red fan-shaped flower inside them. The pieces with grapes have two rosettes filling in the space at the larger end; the other pieces have three rosettes as space fillers.

Cairo Museum entry no.: 21842.
Height: 7.7 cm. Length: 60 cm.
Provenance: Tell el-Yahudiyah.
Date: New Kingdom, Dynasty 20.

The Ramesside kings lived in a sumptuous palace-city in the Delta called Pi-Ramses Mery-Amun, "House of Ramses, Beloved of Amun." This glazed tile fragment showing a wild duck in a marsh setting was among the tiles found at Qantir. They once covered the palace's floors and lower walls.

The vertical zigzag lines in the background represent water. To the right of the duck is a lily pad and to the left is a lotus. The plumage of the duck is shown in beautiful detail.

Cairo Museum entry no.: 89480.
Length: 18.7 cm. Width: 18.4 cm.
Provenance: Qantir.
Date: New Kingdom, Dynasty 19.

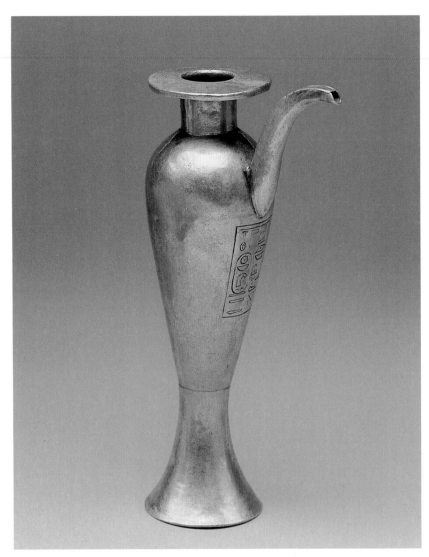

This gold vessel bearing the prenomen of King Ahmose, the first king of the Eighteenth Dynasty, was found in the tomb of Psusennes I at Tanis. It must have originally come from Upper Egypt. The inscription, incised in a rectangle on the front, reads: "The Good God Neb-pehty-Re, Justified, Beloved of Osiris, Lord of Abydos."

Because the inscription names the god Osiris, god of the underworld, this piece may have been made for the cult of Osiris at Abydos or as a funerary piece for King Ahmose.

The vessel is made from four separate pieces soldered together. Seams are visible between the body of the vessel and the foot, at the neck, and at the spout. Vessels of this shape were used for libations, both in temple and funerary rituals.

Cairo Museum entry no.: 85895.
Height: 14.6 cm. Maximum diameter: 5 cm.
Base diameter: 4 cm.
Provenance: Tanis.
Date: New Kingdom, Dynasty 18.

This alabaster vessel, found at the tomb of Merneptah, son of Ramses II, in the Valley of the Kings, was either part of the king's funerary equipment or held a substance used in his embalming. It was buried near the tomb entrance with the other embalming materials.

Inscribed on the body of the vessel are the prenomen and nomen of the king. A cartouche encircles each of the names. The hieroglyphs have been carved into the alabaster and then inlaid with red and blue paste. They read: "Lord of the Two Lands, User-ma'at-Re, Setep-en-Re, Lord of Appearances, Ramses, Beloved of Amun."

On the side of the alabastron is a secondary hieratic inscription in black ink. The lid stopper is missing.

Cairo Museum entry no.: 46712.
Height: 26.6 cm.
Provenance: Thebes.
Date: New Kingdom, Dynasty 19.

This tall-necked gold vessel was found in the tomb of King Psusennes I at Tanis (see also objects 18 and 48). The style of the vessel is extremely simple and elegant. The only decoration is on the spout, which has been incised to represent a flaring papyrus umbel. Just below the shoulder of the vessel the prenomen and nomen of Psusennes appear. This vessel was used to pour water over the king's hands, probably into a gold basin (see object 15).

Cairo Museum entry no.: 85892.
Height: 38 cm.
Maximum diameter: 8.9 cm.
Provenance: Tanis.
Date: Third Intermediate Period, Dynasty 21.

This gold basin was found in the tomb of King Psusennes I at Tanis. It would have been held under the hands of the king while water was poured over them from a matching gold vessel (see object 14). The basin is very simple in form. The only decoration is the lotus blossom handle, which was made separately and riveted to the basin in three places. Opposite the handle the cartouches of Psusennes I have been stamped on the side of the basin.

Cairo Museum entry no.: 85893.
Height: 17 cm. Diameter: 10.2 cm.
Provenance: Tanis.
Date: Third Intermediate Period, Dynasty 21.

This clepsydra, or water clock, is an open alabaster vessel deeply incised with texts and scenes on the exterior that would have originally been inlaid with faience and carnelian. It was found, broken into pieces, in the Karnak cachette, buried in the Court of the Seventh Pylon of the Karnak Temple.

Whereas the exterior of the clock has a series of inscriptions and scenes, the interior is marked only by two alternating hieroglyphic signs and a series of dots. At the bottom of one side is a small hole. The water clock was filled to the top at sunset, and when the water dropped to the first appropriate dot for the right season and month, one hour had passed.

This water clock was carved in the reign of Amenhotep III during the later Eighteenth Dynasty. His cartouche can be seen above each of the royal figures on the exterior decoration, which is divided into three registers. The bottom register is divided into six scenes, each of which depicts Amenophis III between two deities. Each of the deities symbolizes one of the months of the year.

In the middle register, over the opening, the circumpolar stars are depicted. The rest of the register is divided into representations of the days of the week. Part of this middle register and part of the one above are decorated with a larger scene of the king making an offering to Re-Horachty, the sun god, while Thoth, the moon god, looks on.

The upper register is decorated with both a list and representations of all the planets and constellations through which the sun god would have to travel. The outer opening at the base of the vessel was originally decorated with a seated baboon, through which the water passed.

Inside the water clock are the alternating hieroglyphic signs *ankh*, "life," and *djed*, "stability." Above each sign is a vertical row of dots. At the top of each row on the rim of the vessel are the names of the seasons and months of the ancient Egyptian calendar.

The ancient Egyptians divided their year of 365 days into three seasons: *akhet*, "inundation," *peret*, "coming forth (of the land)," and *shemu*, "deficiency (of water)." In each season were four months of 30 days each (5 days were added to make the 365-day year), making a twelve-month year. Each day was divided into twenty-four hours, twelve of day and twelve of night.

The calibration marks on the clock's interior show that the shortest time scale was for the second month of deficiency, whereas the longest scale was for the fourth month of inundation.

Cairo Museum entry no.: 37525.
Exterior height: 35 cm.
Maximum upper diameter: 49 cm.
Maximum lower diameter: 27.5 cm.
Rim thickness: 2 cm.
Provenance: Thebes.
Date: New Kingdom, Dynasty 18.

These faience tiles were inlaid with glass paste colors, some of which have fallen out. The representation on them is both decorative and symbolic, for each of the three separate parts of the design is also a hieroglyphic sign. The birds are plovers, *Vanellus cristatus*, called *rekhyet* in ancient Egyptian. They sit, with lifted wings and raised legs, on *neb*-baskets inlaid with either alternating red and blue checks or checks in various shades of blue.

In front of the body of each bird is a five-pointed star. Arms raised in adoration to this star form the hieroglyphic word *dua*, "adore." *Rekhyet* was the ancient word for "people," and *neb* the adjective "all." This design can then be read as the phrase "all the people adore," referring, of course, to adoring the king. Note the multicolor inlay in the wings of the bird to the far left.

These tiles are from the mortuary temple of Ramses III at Medinet Habu on the West Bank of Thebes. Tiles of similar design were also found at the Ramesside palace at Qantir.

Cairo Museum entry no.: 33968.
Provisional catalog no.: 5–2–24–7.
Larger tile: Length: 23.1 cm. Width: 11 cm.
Thickness: 2 cm.
Smaller tile: Length: 7.8 cm. Width: 12 cm.
Thickness: 2 cm.
Provenance: Thebes.
Date: New Kingdom, Dynasty 20.

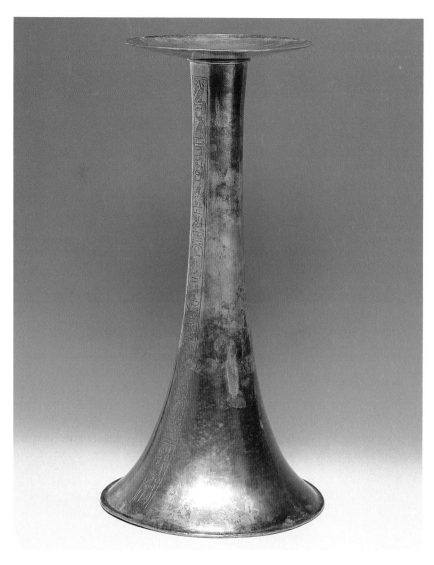

This silver offering stand with dish was found in the tomb of Psusennes I at Tanis. The sunken center of the dish inserts securely into the open top of the stand.

This piece was probably made for use in the funerary ritual of the king, since the gods invoked in the inscriptions are funerary deities. The vertical inscription on the stand gives the titulary of the king and says that he is "Beloved of Osiris, Lord of Eternity," and "Wen-nofer, Ruler of the Living." The titulary of the king appears again on the dish, and here the god Ptah-Sokar-Osiris is invoked.

Cairo Museum entry no.: 86899.
Height: 59.5 cm. Diameter at base: 8.5 cm.
Depth of dish: 8 cm. Top diameter: 25.7 cm.
Provenance: Tanis.
Date: Third Intermediate Period,
Dynasty 21.

This small sandstone statue came from the so-called Karnak cachette, a collection of statuary and other pieces taken from Karnak Temple in ancient times and reburied in the Court of the Seventh Pylon. The statue depicts Ramses II as a sphinx, presenting the vessel of Amun.

This vessel, typically made of gold or silver, held Nile waters taken from the beginning of the inundation. It was presented as an offering to the god Amun at the New Year's Festival.

The Egyptian New Year, heralded by the heliacal rising of the Dog Star, Sirius, began in midsummer, approximately the same time that the Nile began to rise with the yearly flood. The statue was originally painted, and it is possible the vessel was gilded.

This manner of depicting the king as a crouching sphinx is a traditional pose known from the Old Kingdom. Ramses wears the *nemes*-headcloth with uraeus and a false beard. Usually the only human part of a sphinx is the head, but here the arms of the king are represented as well, holding forth the vessel of Amun. Incised on the front of the vessel are the prenomen and nomen of the king in cartouches.

Cairo Museum entry no.: 38060.
Museum catalog no.: 42146.
Height: 18 cm. Length: 37 cm. Width: 9 cm.
Provenance: Thebes.

This small schist statue of Ramses II, found in the cachette at Karnak Temple (see also object 19), depicts the king prostrate, offering a box containing a ritual vessel to the god Amun. In front of the box a small offering table is carved on the base of the statue.

Ramses is wearing the royal headcloth, the *nemes*-headcloth, and the royal kilt. The piece was badly damaged in antiquity and has been restored, but enough of the base remains to see that the king is kneeling on the branches and leaves of the *ished*-tree. This tree, the persea, was the holy tree that grew in the temple at Heliopolis. At the time of their coronations, the names of each king were ritually inscribed on its leaves. The names of Ramses II are inscribed on the leaves just behind his bent leg. In the inscription that runs along both sides of the base, Ramses has included in his titulary the phrase "his deeds are established hundreds of thousands of times upon the *ished*-tree."

Cairo Museum entry no.: 37423.
Museum catalog no.: 42142.
Height: 27.5 cm. Length: 75.8 cm.
Width: 12.5 cm.
Provenance: Thebes.
Date: New Kingdom, Dynasty 19.

Before a body was embalmed, the vital organs were removed and mummified separately. Then they were placed in jars, called canopic jars (see also object 56). In royal burials the viscera were first placed in small anthropoid, or human-shaped, coffins and then placed within canopic jars. The funeral rites for Sen-nedjem, a workman for the pharaoh, seem to follow this royal tradition, for here we have a small limestone canopic coffin, carved in two halves, from his tomb at Deir el-Medina.

The body of the figure is painted white, as if wrapped in linen, and yellow bands outlined in red secure the wrappings. Each yellow band has an inscription in black. Down the front of the mummy figure are the titles and name of Sen-nedjem; on the sides are protective spells said by funerary deities and representations of the cardinal points.

The heavy stripes on the mummy's head are painted in imitation of the gold and lapis lazuli found on a royal headdress. A broad bead necklace is below the throat, and a lotus petal necklace covers the chest. On a royal coffin the wings of the vulture that protected the deceased appeared on the chest.

Cairo Museum entry no.: SR41=C4251.
Height: 34 cm.
Provenance: Thebes.
Date: New Kingdom, Dynasty 19.

This wooden shawabti box is in the form of the Palace of the North, the residence of the prehistoric kings of Lower Egypt. It is a structure characterized by a barrel-vaulted roof between vertical boards. A number of the shawabti or funerary figures of Kha-bekhnet, the son of Sen-nedjem, would have stood inside. This box, along with at least three others belonging to Kha-bekhnet, was found in the tomb of Sen-nedjem at Deir el-Medina.

The box rests on a base with two sledge runners. A full-sized chest, like one for royal canopic jars, would have been dragged to the tomb on its runners. Obviously, this one could have been carried.

The wooden box has been stuccoed and painted. The colors (blue, green, and red on a yellow ground), as well as the striping, are conventional in representing the Palace of the North. The knobs on the lid and the front side are for tying the box shut. The vertical line of inscription in black ink down the front reads: "Revered with Osiris, Kha-bekhnet, Justified."

Cairo Museum entry no.: J27296.
Height: 30 cm.
Provenance: Thebes.
Date: New Kingdom, Dynasty 19.

This wooden door is one of the few surviving from ancient Egypt, and of those the best preserved. It was still in place, closing off the burial chamber of Sen-nedjem at Deir el-Medina, when the tomb was opened in 1886. The door itself is made from five curved panels of wood held together by a frame on the top and bottom. The door was stuccoed, then painted with one rectangular scene on each side. A block of wood with two metal rings on the outside of the door held the bolt by which the door was fastened.

Two registers are painted on the outside of the door. In the upper one the god Osiris sits with the goddess *Ma'at,* "Truth," behind him on the left. Osiris, wrapped as a mummy, holds the crook and flail, the symbols of kingship, in his hands, as well as the *was-*scepter, the scepter signifying dominion. On his head is the festive *atef*-crown. The green color of Osiris' face indicates his position as a god of fertility.

Adoring the god are Sen-nedjem, his wife Iy-nefer, and their daughter Nefer. Sen-nedjem wears a long pleated linen kilt, and the women have full-length, pleated linen gowns. All three have incense cones on their heads, and the women carry long-necked jugs with liquid offerings for Osiris.

Note the difference in skin color between Sen-nedjem and the female members of his family. By convention females were always shown light skinned, not tanned by having to be out in the sun. They are also all barefoot, a sign of respect in the presence of a god.

Below, the sons of Sen-nedjem adore the god Ptah-Sokar-Osiris, who is attended by the goddess Isis. This composite god, tying together the two Memphite cults of Ptah and Sokar with the funerary cult of Osiris, was very popular in the New Kingdom. He is shown with a falcon head, since Sokar was a falcon. He holds the symbol "life" in his right hand and the *was*-scepter in his left. The first son has his hands up in adoration, whereas the others, in pairs, hold a floral offering in one hand and show adoration with the other. The first son is Kha-bekhnet (see objects 22 and 34), the fourth son is Khonsu (see object 24), and the fifth son in line is Ramose (see object 29).

On the inside of the door, the side which would have faced the burial chamber, Sen-nedjem and his wife Iy-nefer sit while he plays *senet* (see object 52). In front of them are food, drink, and bouquets, offered for the funeral feast. The text under this scene comes from the end of Spell 72 of the Book of the Dead and is followed by the opening of Spell 17 (see object 24) in the last four vertical columns. Spell 72 is to help the deceased in penetrating the underworld and ascending to the *sekhet yaru,* the Field of Rushes in the afterlife. Spell 17 is one recited by the deceased as he sits in a pavilion playing senet. It assures that Sen-nedjem becomes a "living soul" after death.

Cairo Museum entry no.: 27303.
Height: 1.35 m. Width: 78 cm.
Provenance: Thebes.
Date: New Kingdom, Dynasty 19.

This rectangular, wooden sarcophagus of Khonsu contained the inner human-shaped coffins in which his mummy was placed. This outer sarcophagus and its inner coffins were found in the tomb of his father, Sen-nedjem, at Deir el-Medina. Constructed from pieces of wood that were stuccoed, painted, and varnished, the side and top pieces were made to be assembled over and around the mummy already laid on the bottom piece.

This sarcophagus imitates a royal sarcophagus of stone. Its shape is that of the Palace of the South (see object 60), the residence of prehistoric kings of Upper Egypt. This type of structure is characterized by a bulging roof over one end and, below the edge of the roof, a decorative cavetto cornice with striped vertical lines. The bottom of the sarcophagus has two sledge runners on which it was dragged to the tomb.

All four sides of the sarcophagus are decorated with texts and scenes from the Book of the Dead, a collection of spells to insure the resurrection of the deceased in the afterlife. On front and back are four goddesses, two at each end. Isis and Nephthys are on the back, and Selket and Neith are on the front, shown here. The goddesses stand back to back facing the words they would recite on behalf of the deceased. Each goddess, her name written on her head, wears a beautifully embroidered sheath dress.

The text on both long sides is that of chapter one of the Book of the Dead. This opening spell was to assure the descent of the deceased into the west. Bracketing the scenes above are ibis-headed spirits, each holding a scepter topped with the hieroglyphic for "heaven." The spirit of the north brackets each side at one end and the spirit of the south each side at the other. In front of each of these spirits is one of the four sons of Horus: Imsety with a man's head, Hapy with a baboon head, Kebsennuef with a falcon head, and Duamutef with a dog's head.

On one side of the sarcophagus in the center top are two lions back to back. The hieroglyphic symbol for "horizon" is between them, and the symbol for "life" hangs from it. Khonsu is worshipping the lion on the right, who is labeled the "sun god Re" in the inscription. The other lion looks toward a falcon head, the god Horus, who is protected by a reclining cow symbolizing the goddess Hathor. The cow and falcon are on a rectangle marked with zigzag lines for water. The inscription above says that "Horus is arising from the primeval waters." This is an illustration of Spell 71 of the Book of the Dead, in which the deceased asks for help from the "falcon who rises from the deep."

In the scene below, the two goddesses Isis and Nephthys kneel at either end of a canopy. Inside, the jackal-headed god Anubis is attending the mummy of the deceased, which lies on a lion-headed bed. To the left, the spirits of the deceased and his wife, both shown in the form of the *ba*-bird, sit with food offerings heaped before them.

On top of the opposite side of the sarcophagus is a representation of the Palace of the North (see object 22), with two deities on either side. To the left sit two of the sons of Horus holding the symbol for "life." On the right are two fleshy and overweight male figures. This is the traditional way the god of the Nile, or the flood, is shown. The larger figure on the right holds two sticks that are the hieroglyphic signs for "year" while his hand is over some kind of egg. The other figure stands with his hands over two basins of water, probably an illustration of Spell 17, which talks about the deceased "being cleansed in two ponds" and Re being "born from the Great Flood."

Below, Khonsu and his wife Tamaket are playing the board game senet (see object 52) in a pavilion. On the left side Khonsu is worshipping the goddess Hathor, who is called "Mistress of Heaven" in the inscription. Three eyes of Horus hover over these scenes. These again are vignettes from Spell 17, the spell to be recited by "one playing senet in a pavilion after death."

On one side of the top of the coffin sit two jackals on shrines, representing the god Anubis. On the other side the sky goddess, Nut, stretches out. Below and beside her are *wadjet*-eyes, symbols of the protective eye of the god Horus.

Cairo Museum entry no.: 27302.
Height: 1.25 m. Length, including runner: 2.62 m. Width: 98 cm.
Provenance: Thebes.
Date: New Kingdom, Dynasty 19.

This outer coffin encased the mummy of the workman Sen-nedjem, and inside was another lid, or cover-board, over the actual mummy (see object 26). Although the inner cover-board presents Sen-nedjem as a living person, the outer coffin depicts him as a mummy.

Details such as the hands were made separately and set into the stuccoed, painted, and varnished wood. Sen-nedjem wears a short false beard and has a garland of flowers over his elaborate wig. The goddess Nephthys is represented above his head and the goddess Isis at his feet. Both are protectors of the deceased.

Sen-nedjem holds the *tyit,* or knot of Isis, in his left hand and the *djed*-pillar of Osiris in his right. On his chest lies a broad beaded collar and a larger, wider floral necklace.

The coffin is divided by vertical and horizontal bands of inscription imitating the wrappings of the mummy. On the coffin sides are scenes depicting the funerary deities known as the four sons of Horus. On the top, below Sen-nedjem's arms, the goddess Nut spreads her protective wings.

The first of three pairs of scenes along the body depicts Anubis, the jackal god of the dead, seated on a shrine. In the next a goddess kneels, protecting the *shen*-sign, which means to "encircle" or to "enclose," referring to protection of the mummy. In the last scene, Sen-nedjem kneels below a sycamore tree receiving libations from the goddess within.

Cairo Museum entry no.: 27308.
Length: 1.85 m. Width: 50 cm.
Provenance: Thebes.
Date: New Kingdom, Dynasty 19.

This is the inner lid or cover-board for the mummy of Sen-nedjem. Depicting him as he was when alive, the cover-board lay on top of the mummy and was enclosed within the outer coffin (see object 25). Sen-nedjem wears the same type of wig and beard shown on the outer coffin, but the wig is undecorated and the broad collar is much smaller and simpler. Sen-nedjem wears a long, pleated linen kilt, and his arms, decorated only with bracelets, hang down in front.

In the space between his legs, a vertical inscription reads: "The Servant of the Place of Truth upon the West of Thebes, Sen-nedjem, Justified." "Servant" was the title given all the workmen at Deir el-Medina, and the "Place of Truth" was the name given the Valley of the Kings in which they worked.

This cover-board, like the outer coffin, is made of stuccoed and painted wood. It was restored in 1975. The only funerary decoration on the piece is the figure of the goddess Isis below the feet.

Cairo Museum entry no.: 27308.
Length: 1.75 m. Width: 44.3 cm.
Provenance: Thebes.
Date: New Kingdom, Dynasty 19.

Isis, the "Mistress of the House," was the wife of Kha-bekhnet, one of the sons of Sen-nedjem. Her mummy and accompanying funerary equipment were found in the tomb of Sen-nedjem at Deir el-Medina along with those of her husband. This wooden cover-board, which represents Isis as in life, lay over her mummy. The wood has been covered with stucco and then with linen painted predominately white, red, green, and yellow.

Isis wears a long wig with a wide headband and pendant lotus blossoms over her forehead. Through her hair on each side of her face protrude two earrings, one a ring and the other a button. A broad bead collar covers her chest, and rosette designs are over her breasts. Isis wears a full-length, pleated linen gown with full sleeves. One arm is across her chest while the other lies flat along her body. Four different bracelets are on each arm, and on her right hand are four rings.

The whiteness of her linen gown is accented by the green cluster of leaves she grasps in her left hand and holds against her body with her right. The inscription between her feet gives her name and states that she is revered under the god Osiris. Under her feet is a drawing of the goddess Isis. Around the edge of the cover-board is a funerary inscription.

Cairo Museum entry no.: 27309.
Length: 1.93 m. Width: 47 cm.
Provenance: Thebes.
Date: New Kingdom, Dynasty 19.

This wooden cover-board, stuccoed and painted, once lay over the mummy of the "Chief Merchant of the Prince, Piay." Although not depicted as a mummy, Piay is in typical mummy position with hands crossed on his chest. Originally he must have held the *tyit*-knot of Isis and the *djed*-pillar of Osiris in his hands. He wears a full-length linen gown with pleated sleeves and a linen shawl tied around his middle that falls in a pleated apron down his front. Below is the vertical inscription giving his name and title.

Piay's wig is similar to the one on Sen-nedjem's cover-board, although Piay wears an elaborate floral headband. He also has two bracelets on each arm and wears round earrings. A drop-shaped mark on his abdomen indicates the depression of the navel below.

Cairo Museum provisional catalog no.: 5–12–25–3.
Length: 1.79 m. Width: 43 cm.
Provenance: Thebes.
Date: New Kingdom, Dynasty 19.

This shawabti, or funerary figure, of Ramose came from the tomb of his father, Sen-nedjem, at Deir el-Medina. The inscription down the middle of the figure reads: "The Osiris, Child of the Tomb, Ramose, Justified." The title "Child of the Tomb" was applied to a young boy in the community of Deir el-Medina who was expected to grow up and become a workman in the royal tombs. Ramose apparently died as a youth, however, for he never attained the position of workman.

Carved from a piece of limestone, this painted shawabti displays a white shroud from which the feet protrude. The figure wears a long wig topped with a floral headband. The hands are crossed on the chest in mummiform style. In each hand is a hoe for laboring in the afterlife.

Cairo Museum entry no.: J27232.
Museum catalog no.: 47765.
Height: 19 cm.
Provenance: Thebes.
Date: New Kingdom, Dynasty 19.

Although it is also carved of limestone and painted, this shawabti of
the Deir el-Medina workman Sen-
nedjem is much more traditional in
shape and style than that of his son
Ramose (see object 29). The wig is
in the typical, heavy tripartite
style, with the ears sticking out in
front. The body of the figure is
painted white, indicating that a
linen cloak or shroud is wrapped
around it. The arms are crossed on
the chest, each hand holding a hoe.
An elaborate broad collar is carefully depicted on the chest. The
colors of the detail stand out
beautifully against the pure white
of the body.

The eight lines of horizontal
inscription on the figure give
Spell 6 of the Book of the Dead.
This spell insures that the shawabti
will come alive and perform chores
required of the deceased in the
afterlife.

Cairo Museum entry no.: 27251.
Museum catalog no.: 47740.
Height: 29 cm.
Provenance: Thebes.
Date: New Kingdom, Dynasty 19.

This lamp was found in the tomb of the workman Kha at Deir el-Medina. He lived during the reigns of the Eighteenth Dynasty pharaohs Tuthmosis IV and Amenophis III. The lamp might have been placed in the tomb as a piece Kha had used at home during his lifetime, or it might have been left burning in the tomb at the time of burial to help illuminate the underworld for the deceased.

The lamp stands on a limestone base and is held up by a wooden column in the shape of a papyrus stalk. On top of the papyrus flower three wooden sticks support the bronze bowl of the lamp, which has a handle at one end and a pointed pouring spout at the other. The bowl still contains a whitish substance, the remains of burnt material, and a small wooden stick. The lamp's twisted linen wick would have been fueled by a vegetable oil, with salt added to keep the oil from smoking.

Cairo Museum entry no.: 38642.
Total height: 1.05 m. Base height: 8 cm.
Base diameter: 26.5 cm.
Lamp height: 7 cm. Total length: 24.5 cm.
Width: 18.1 cm.
Provenance: Thebes.
Date: New Kingdom, Dynasty 18.

This small pottery jar came from the tomb of Sen-nedjem at Deir el-Medina. It has been thrown on a potter's wheel from a fine buff clay. The body of the jar is oval, with a lug handle on each shoulder. The neck is straight and tall, ending in a square lip.

The jar has been painted with a series of floral friezes in light and dark green, with details in white and red. The body of the jar displays decoration similar to that on a mummy. A broad collar of lotus petals spreads across the vessel, and a lotus blossom pendant is flanked on each side by a lotus bud and pomegranate. The neck of the jar has a lotus petal frieze around the top and bottom, with a square field painted with mandrake fruits in the middle.

Cairo Museum entry no.: J27216.
Height: 33 cm.
Provenance: Thebes.
Date: New Kingdom, Dynasty 19.

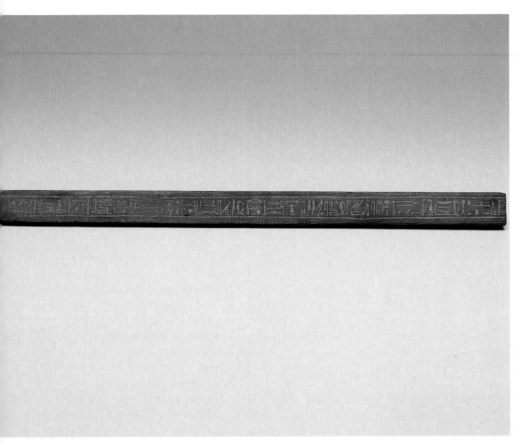

This wooden cubit measuring rod was found in the tomb of Sen-nedjem at Deir el-Medina (see also objects 35 and 37). The basic unit of linear measurement in ancient Egypt, a cubit equaled 52.5 centimeters (20.6 inches), or, according to natural proportions, the distance from the elbow to the tip of the middle finger. On the back of the cubit rod are lines dividing it into smaller units of measure.

A workman like Sen-nedjem would have used this cubit rod to lay out grid patterns for drawing tomb decorations. The inscription on the front side names Sen-nedjem and invokes both the king and the god Ptah, "Lord of Truth" and patron of craftsmen.

Cairo Museum entry no.: 27211.
Length: 52.7 cm.
Provenance: Thebes.
Date: New Kingdom, Dynasty 19.

This wooden box carries the names of Kha-bekhnet, son of Sen-nedjem, and his wife Sahti. It was found in the tomb of Sen-nedjem at Deir el-Medina. Because Kha-bekhnet is referred to as an Osiris and his wife as justified, we know this object was made for their burial and not for use during their lifetime.

The rectangular box rests on four short legs, one of which is restored. The box has a flat lid that opens on one side. There is a knob on the lid and another on the side for tying and sealing the box. Inside, it is divided into compartments, probably meant to hold jewelry. Painted white decorations, imitating ivory inlay, and red detail adorn the exterior.

The inscription on the lid reads: "The Osiris, the Servant in the Place of Truth, Kha-bekhnet, His Wife, the Mistress of the House, Sahti, Justified, Happy and in Peace."

Cairo Museum entry no.: 27292.
Length: 28 cm. Width: 20 cm.
Height: 17 cm.
Provenance: Thebes.
Date: New Kingdom, Dynasty 19.

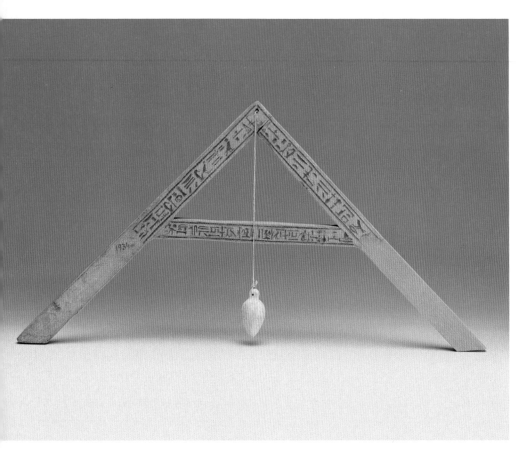

This level, along with a vertical level (see object 37) and a cubit measuring stick, was found in the tomb of Sen-nedjem at Deir el-Medina. The three pieces that make up the level are wood, and the plumb bob is limestone. The right diagonal piece of the level was broken away; when it was restored in 1975, a string was added to suspend the bob.

The level is constructed of two diagonal pieces of wood joined at a right angle, with a short horizontal piece running between these two. The plumb bob hangs from the top of the right angle. When the level is placed on a flat surface, the plumb bob hangs exactly in the middle of the marks incised in the center of the horizontal piece.

The inscription on the horizontal piece is divided into two halves that read toward the middle from each end, both ending with the words "Sen-nedjem, Justified." The inscriptions on the two diagonals invoke the gods Ptah and Re-Horachty-Atum.

Cairo Museum entry no.: 27258.
Length of diagonal: 36.3 cm.
Length of horizontal: 22.2 cm.
Height of bob: 5.3 cm.
Provenance: Thebes.
Date: New Kingdom, Dynasty 19.

In nonroyal burials sometimes an expensive item was imitated in an inexpensive medium such as wood or pottery. This pottery vessel from Sen-nedjem's tomb at Deir el-Medina is an imitation of an alabastron, a pear-shaped alabaster jar. It has been painted white with variegated stripes to imitate alabaster's veined appearance.

The vessel's lid has been painted to resemble the center of a lotus flower. The inscription running vertically down the yellow center band reads: "The Osiris, Servant of the Lord of the Two Lands, Sen-nedjem."

This piece came from the tomb of Sen-nedjem at Deir el-Medina.

Cairo Museum entry no.: 27248.
Height: 14.5 cm.
Provenance: Thebes.
Date: New Kingdom, Dynasty 19.

This plumb level, composed of a wooden support with limestone plumb bob and line, came from the tomb of Sen-nedjem at Deir el-Medina. A workman like Sen-nedjem would have used this instrument to verify that wall faces of corridors and chambers in a royal tomb were precisely vertical. If the plumb line just touched the edge of the support's lower protrusion when its flat side was placed against the wall face, the wall was vertical and ready for decoration.

The inscription on the painted support reads: "Servant of the Lord of the Two Lands, Sen-nedjem, Justified." The string was added when the piece was restored in 1975.

Cairo Museum entry no.: 27260.
Height of level: 48.6 cm. Height of bob: 5 cm.
Provenance: Thebes.
Date: New Kingdom, Dynasty 19.

The architect May is depicted in this grey granite statue. His career began under Ramses II and continued in the reign of his son and successor, Merneptah. May squats with his hands turned palms up in supplication. He wears a kilt tied at the waist that completely covers his legs, its rippling edge running diagonally across his lap. May's wig falls in a triangular shape onto each shoulder, pushing his ears out on both sides. This old-style wig was common on Middle Kingdom statues.

A cartouche of King Merneptah is carved on each shoulder, and a six-line offering inscription on the lap is completed by a single line on the base. The inscription invokes Ptah, god of Memphis and patron god of craftsmen, and not only gives May's name and titles, but those of his father and grandfather as well.

Cairo Museum entry no.: 67878.
Height: 74 cm. Base width: 38.5 cm.
Base depth: 47.3 cm.
Provenance: Memphis.
Date: New Kingdom, Dynasty 19.

This small blue bowl is made of faience, a powdered quartz frit. It was probably molded over a core, painted with decoration, and fired. The decoration both inside and out is in black ink, and the firing has given the bowl a lustrous finish.

The outside of the bowl is painted to portray an open lotus blossom. Inside, three concentric rectangles represent a pond. From each of its corners spring open and closed lotuses, and highly decorative palm leaves grow from the ends. Next to each long side swims a bulti fish, a lotus bud trailing from its mouth. Both the bulti fish and the lotus are symbols of rebirth and resurrection (see also object 6). The pond could also represent the primordial waters out of which life sprang.

This bowl was placed in a tomb at Deir el-Medina, probably filled with a drink for the afterlife.

Cairo Museum entry no.: 63677.
Diameter: 17 cm.
Provenance: Thebes.
Date: New Kingdom, Dynasty 18.

Ancient Egyptians used headrests to support their heads while lying on their sides. These seemingly uncomfortable headrests could be made of wood, like this one, or a number of other materials such as pottery, calcite, limestone, or ivory. Not only were these headrests used in the home, but they were also placed in the tomb. A miniature headrest was often put in the mummy wrappings by the neck as well, to protect the head and keep it joined to the body.

Headrests were often decorated with scenes of deities or spells to protect the sleeping person. This one, found at Gurna on the West Bank of Thebes, displays an incised figure of the god Bes, a dwarflike lion. Bes was a domestic deity, particularly associated with women in childbirth. He holds one knife in his hand and one in each foot. His hand rests on the hieroglyphic sign meaning "protection." Snakes are in his mouth, perhaps symbolizing his ability to devour any such creature that might approach the sleeper.

An offering formula is carved on the base, indicating that the headrest was made to be put in the tomb as part of the funerary equipment.

Cairo Museum entry no.: JE6269.
Height: 20 cm. Width: 14 cm.
Length: 36 cm.
Provenance: Thebes.
Date: New Kingdom.

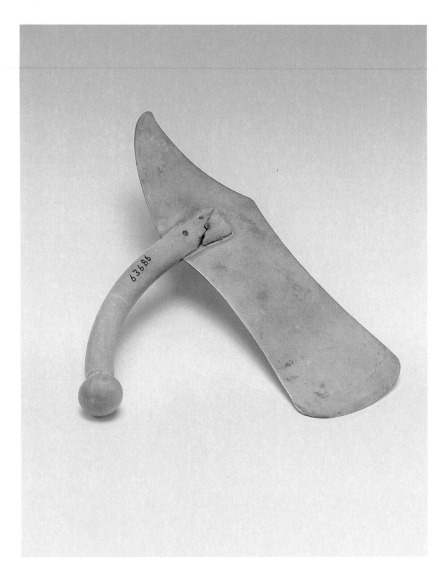

Razors from prehistoric times in Egypt were simply sharpened rectangular pieces of flint used as scrapers. By the Old Kingdom there were metal, spatula-shaped razors. In the New Kingdom the razor had further developed into the five-sided form we see in this one found at Deir el-Medina on the West Bank of Thebes.

This razor consists of a bronze blade riveted to a wooden handle that curves toward the cutting end of the blade. The larger, rounded sharp edge is balanced on the other end by a pointed tang or spur, which may also have helped in manipulating the razor.

Cairo Museum entry no.: 63686.
Length: 16.6 cm.
Provenance: Thebes.
Date: New Kingdom.

Ostracon (plural *ostraca*) is the name applied to an inscribed potsherd or limestone chip. Since papyrus was a fairly valuable commodity, ostraca were used the same as notepads or tablets for sketches, memos, lists, dates, etc. Many ostraca with drawings have been found in association with the workmen's village at Deir el-Medina. The artists of this community practiced drawings on ostraca before decorating the wall of a royal tomb or temple, or they would simply sketch for their own amusement.

This ostracon found in the Valley of the Kings depicts a ram, the sacred animal of the god Amun of Thebes. In front of the ram are food and floral offerings. Above the picture the inscription reads: "Amun-Re, the Ram, This God Who Is over the Gods." Down the left side of the ostracon the artist has indicated under whom he works: "The Great One of the Crew Is Hay."

The foreman of the crew, Hay, is known to have worked at Deir el-Medina from the reign of Merneptah, son of Ramses II, until well into the reign of Ramses III of the Twentieth Dynasty.

Cairo Museum entry no.: 23−2−22−1.
Height: 11 cm. Width: 18 cm.
Provenance: Thebes.
Date: New Kingdom, Dynasty 19 or 20.

This limestone chip (or ostracon) painted with the picture of a harpist was found in the workmen's village of Deir el-Medina on the West Bank of Thebes. A man shown with exaggerated arms and fingers is plucking a twelve-string harp. The harp is of the arched type, with a boat-shaped sound box typical of the New Kingdom. The tuning pegs are painted alternating red and black, and the sound box is decorated, perhaps to represent leatherwork.

The bald harpist is wearing a simple diadem and a long linen gown typical of the Ramesside Period. There are many lines around his neck, perhaps indicating rolls of fat. Although harpists in ancient Egypt were often represented as being blind, in this drawing it is not clear whether he is blind or not. In the Amarna Period blind harpists are shown playing in part of the temple ritual. Since they would be coming face-to-face with the deity, they are symbolically blind and therefore unable to look upon the god.

This ostracon was possibly the practice piece for a scene accompanying what is called the "Harper's Song," a song or poem for the deceased reflecting on and praising death and the tomb. This type of text, found on tomb walls and stelae, is always accompanied by the depiction of a harpist.

Cairo Museum entry no.: 69409.
Height: 13.8 cm. Width: 11 cm.
Provenance: Thebes.
Date: New Kingdom, Dynasty 19 or 20.

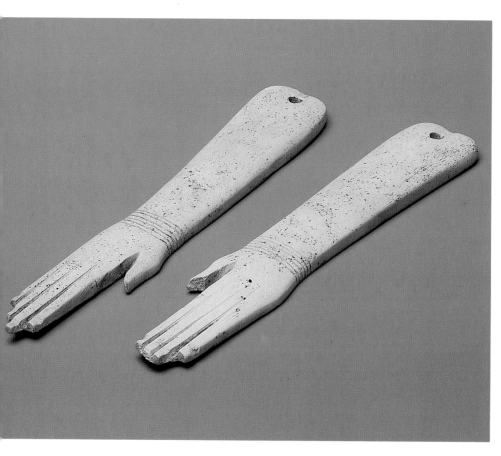

Clappers made of wood, bone, or ivory were musical instruments generally used by women, particularly dancing girls. The two pieces were tied together through holes at the ends and then shaken so the flat sides would clap together.

Clappers are always shaped like human forearms, either straight, as in this pair, or curved. They generally end in hands, although more elaborate clappers end with lotus flowers or human or animal heads.

There are lines representing bracelets on these bone (?) clapper arms, and grooves have been worn by the strings that once held them together.

Cairo Museum entry no.: 25820.
Museum catalog no.: 69211.
Length: 17.5 cm.
Provenance: Thebes.
Date: New Kingdom.

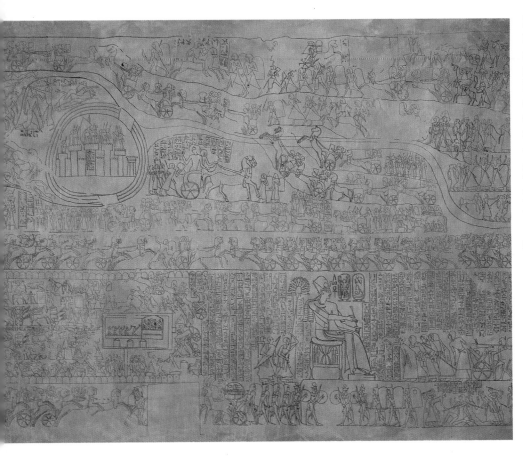

In the fifth year of his reign, Ramses II led a large army to Syria to reassert Egyptian authority in that disputed region. The Hittite Empire, reaching eastward and southward from what is modern-day Turkey, sent a sizable force under the emperor Muwatallis to defeat the youthful Egyptian leader and check his expansionist plans. The two armies came together at Kadesh, a strongly fortified city on the Orontes River.

The Hittites lulled the Egyptian forces into an ambush with false spies captured by the Egyptians, and only by Ramses' personal valor and the timely arrival of an Egyptian support force was total defeat averted. Rallying his battered and beleaguered forces, Ramses turned the tide of the battle and even salvaged a measure of triumph and personal honor. The next day the armies met head-on and fought to a stalemate.

Accounts of the battle were inscribed on numerous monuments in Egypt. This account from the Ramses Temple at Abu Simbel, reproduced here by BYU artist Franz M. Johansen, is perhaps the best known.   —C.W.G.

This limestone relief depicts part of the procession of the "Beautiful Festival of the Valley."

In the upper register the portable bark of Amun, bearing the veiled shrine with the deity's image, is being carried by priests out of a chapel or way station. Ramses II is in front, facing the procession. Instead of a crown, he wears a short wig with uraeus. He has an elaborate two-layer linen gown with decorated apron. The king holds out an incense brazier with falcon handle in his left hand and tosses balls of incense into the flames with his right.

The bark is carried on the shoulders of twenty-four priests, and the bow and stern of the bark are decorated with the ram head of Amun wearing a broad collar and sun disc. Around the shrine in the center are statuettes of divinities and of the king. These would have been cast of precious materials and set into the wooden bark. Priests wearing leopard skins accompany the procession, and another man, named Ipuy, is holding one scepter with a lotus blossom and another with an ostrich feather.

Following the procession is the "Vizier of the South, Paser," with the "King's Scribe, Amenemope," behind him. In the broken register below, Amenemope is shown again, kneeling in adoration of the Amun bark, "User-het." The seven lines of vertical inscription in between give Amenemope's prayer to Amun for personal salvation.

Cairo Museum entry no.: 43591.
Approximate height: 60 cm.
Approximate width: 80 cm.
Provenance: Thebes.
Date: New Kingdom, Dynasty 19.

Six painted sandstone statues once stood in an open-air sun sanctuary on the north side of the entrance to the Temple of Ramses II at Abu Simbel in Nubia. Four of these statues, the baboons shown here, were originally on an altar fronted by two obelisks. The standing baboons, representing the spirit of the god Thoth, hailed the sun as it rose and set.

On the north side of this altar stood a small unroofed naos, or shrine, that contained the other two statues, a seated baboon and a scarab beetle. The baboon represents Thoth, the moon god, and wears the moon disc on its head and a pendant with a winged scarab beetle on its chest. The scarab, on the other hand, represents the sun god Re-Horachty and carries the sun disc with uraeus on its back. The scarab symbolizes rebirth and resurrection and in this context represents the rebirth of the sun after twelve hours of darkness.

The seated baboon and scarab are now set in a modern model of the original shrine. On each side of the open door the titles of Ramses are given in a vertical inscription. In relief on the north side of the shrine, Ramses II is shown offering to the moon god Thoth, and on the south side the king is shown offering to the sun god Re-Horachty.

Cairo Museum entry no.: 42955.
Height of baboons: 92 cm to 99 cm.
Base lengths: 37–43 cm.
Base widths: 26–28 cm.
Height of seated baboon: 92 cm.
Base width: 33 cm.
Height of scarab: 69 cm. Width: 43 cm.
Provenance: Abu Simbel.
Date: New Kingdom, Dynasty 19.

This gold collar was one of six found on the mummy of King Psusennes I in his tomb at Tanis in the Delta. Its style developed from the New Kingdom *shebyu*-collar, a single row of gold beads given by the king to honored high officials. Originally Psusennes' collar comprised six rows of tightly packed disc beads, but now there are only five. In its present mounting it weighs approximately nineteen pounds.

A decorative inscription has been incised on the clasp and inlaid with lapis lazuli. In the center are the king's prenomen and nomen in cartouches, separated by a papyrus column. Above and below are rows of uraei with sun discs, and at the top is a winged beetle holding a sun disc. From this clasp hang fourteen gold chains with flower pendants, all of which act as a counterweight for the five rows of gold discs.

Cairo Museum entry no.: 85571.
Total height: 64.5 cm.
Opening diameter: 13.5 cm.
Chain length: 30.7 cm.
Height of clasp: 10.9 cm.
Width of clasp: 7.3 cm.
Provenance: Tanis.
Date: Third Intermediate Period, Dynasty 21.

This pair of gold bracelets bearing the throne name of Ramses II was part of a treasure hoard found at ancient Bubastis in the Egyptian Delta (see also objects 51, 64, and 67). The bracelets are made of hinged halves that fasten with a sliding pin. A piece of lapis lazuli set in the upper side of each bracelet serves as the common body for the two geese.

Gold granules and gold wire, either plain, twisted, or beaded, form the decorative details on the geese. Smooth zigzag lines symbolize water. In a rectangular band near the hinge is the pharaoh's prenomen, "User-ma'at-Re Setep-en-Re," preceded by the title "Lord of the Two Lands" and followed by the phrase "Like Re." At the other end, below the tail of the geese, granules form diamond- and circle-shaped designs.

Ramses II had these bracelets made to adorn a cult statue within the Temple of Bubastis. Perhaps the goose was chosen to decorate the bracelets because it was the most common bird offered as food in temple and funerary rituals.

Cairo Museum entry no.: 39873.
Museum catalog nos.: 52575 and 52576.
Maximum width: 6 cm.
Maximum diameter: 6.5 cm.
Provenance: Bubastis.
Date: New Kingdom, Dynasty 19.

This larger-than-life red granite statue depicts Ramses II bearing the religious standards of the war god Montu and his consort, Rat-tawy.

The king is shown striding with left foot forward, the traditional pose of a standing male figure. He wears the royal *shendjet*-kilt, its panel adorned with a leopard head and a row of uraei at the bottom. Ramses wears a false beard with chin straps and a heavy, short wig with uraeus, or rearing cobra, over his forehead. Supported along the king's arms are two standards resting on the statue's base. The standard of Montu, topped by a falcon with disc, is on his right, and the standard of Rat-tawy, topped by a female head with disc and horns, is on his left. The inscription on the Montu standard states that Ramses made this "as a monument for his father, Montu," and the inscription on the other standard states that he made it "as a monument for his mother, Rat-tawy."

The pharaoh's titles are inscribed on the base, and his name is on his belt. His titulary is repeated again on the full-length dorsal pillar, which serves to prevent breakage, especially at the neck. The hole visible on the top of the king's wig was used to secure a crown made of precious materials.

Cairo Museum entry no.: 44668.
Height: 2.44 m. Width: 1 m.
Base: 73 cm × 1.03 m.
Provenance: Armant.
Date: New Kingdom, Dynasty 19.

This silver jug came from a treasure hoard found at Bubastis in the Delta (see also objects 49, 64, and 67). The jug's shape is reminiscent of the silver pomegranate vessel from the tomb of Tutankhamun, and the vertical rows of hearts may be imitations of pomegranate seeds. The pomegranate originally came into Egypt from Syro-Palestine in the New Kingdom. Since there are a number of foreign elements in the jug's decoration, the artist may have deliberately chosen an alien fruit for his pattern.

Gold sheeting covers the jug's lip, and the goat-shaped handle is also of gold. The goat was crafted in two sections and joined together. The details of its body, tail, horns, and ears were made separately and then attached. The handle is fastened at the top with two gold rivets and at the feet by soldering.

Two horizontal registers run completely around the neck. The lower register pictures fishing and fowling in the marshes, and the upper register wildlife in the desert. The pairs of animals fighting or mating in the upper register are divided by decorative palmettes. Also shown is the mythical winged griffin, which often appears with typical desert animals in ancient Egyptian art.

The inscription that runs around the vessel's shoulder gives blessings for the *ka*, or soul, of the "Royal Butler, Temet-ta-neb." At the beginning of the inscription is a small square showing a man in a Ramesside long linen gown adoring a goddess. In front of the goddess is a small offering table. The goddess has the *ankh*-sign for "life" in one hand and holds a scepter topped with a bird in the other. On the top of her crown is either some type of plant or an odd representation of hair. The identity of the goddess is not known, but she must have been one of the foreign deities whose cult was brought into Egypt during the New Kingdom.

A white lotus blossom is engraved on the bottom of the vessel.

Cairo Museum entry no.: 39867.
Museum catalog no.: 53262.
Height: 16.5 cm. Height of handle: 9.5 cm.
Opening diameter: 8.9 cm.
Provenance: Bubastis.
Date: New Kingdom.

This *senet*-game board with playing pieces came from the Seventeenth Dynasty tomb of Ak-Hor at Dra abu el-Naga on the West Bank of Thebes. The game box is made of ebony and ivory, and the playing pieces are faience. A drawer to store the playing pieces pulls out from one end of the box.

The game of senet dates from the Old Kingdom and was very popular in ancient Egypt. A player won by being the first to move around the thirty squares on the board. Old Kingdom tomb reliefs show two players, but in the New Kingdom only one person is depicted. By this time the game had become symbolic of passing successfully through the underworld, and the player's opponent was an invisible spirit from the netherworld (see also the depictions on objects 23 and 24).

All senet games have three rows of squares, but the decoration on the squares varies with each set. Three squares in the middle of this game board are marked with the Horus falcon, and the sides are inlaid with carved ivory pieces. The decoration that remains shows a human-headed sphinx and one of two original ibexes eating from a palm tree. The motif of animals eating from the "Tree of Life" is well-known in Mesopotamian art.

Cairo Museum entry no.: J21462.
Museum catalog no.: 68005.
Length: 26 cm. Width: 7.6 cm.
Height: 4.7 cm.
Provenance: Thebes.
Date: Second Intermediate Period,
Dynasty 17.

These golden earrings bearing the name of King Seti II were found in Tomb 56 in the Valley of the Kings. Buried with the earrings were a number of other objects belonging to Seti II and his wife Queen Tawosret (see object 67).

On the bar that passes through the ear is a button, or boss, on one end and an open flower with eight petals on the other. Every other petal is embossed with the cartouche of Seti II. The pharaoh's prenomen and nomen are also inscribed on both sides of the trapezoidal piece of gold suspended from the bar. On the bottom of this piece hang seven gold tubes with cornflower pendants.

Earrings were worn by both men and women in the New Kingdom. The mummy of Seti II shows that both his ears had been pierced, so these earrings might have been worn by the king during his lifetime.

Cairo Museum entry no.: 39675.
Museum catalog no.: 52397 and 52398.
Height: 13.5 cm. Length: 5 cm.
Provenance: Thebes.
Date: New Kingdom, Dynasty 19.

This black granite statuary fragment is the upper portion from a seated statue of Ramses II. Although the remains of an inscription on the back pillar do not give the name of the king, stylistically it resembles other statues of Ramses II, particularly his famous seated statue in the Turin Museum.

The king is wearing a short, heavy wig. His own hair is held by a headband that runs across the forehead. A diadem encircles the wig, with a coiled uraeus over the forehead and a uraeus with disc at the end of each streamer.

Ramses wears a tight linen tunic with flaring, pleated sleeves, and pulled over his left shoulder is a pleated shawl. The details of the king's chest have been carefully shown under these layers. His left arm is down, and his right is bent upward holding the *heka*-scepter, the king's crook. On this arm is a wide bracelet decorated with a *wadjet*-eye, the eye of the god Horus. The king also wears a broad collar composed of rows of pendant beads.

Judging from the youthful features of his face, this piece probably dates from very early in the king's reign. The statue has been executed in an extremely delicate style, and the eyes have been lengthened by the cosmetic eye line that extends over the sides of the face. A back pillar comes up just past the neck to prevent breakage.

Cairo Museum catalog no.: 616.
Height: 82.5 cm. Width: 64 cm.
Provenance: Tanis.
Date: New Kingdom, Dynasty 19.

Within two hundred years after Ramses II was buried, his tomb had been looted, and the high priests of Amun rewrapped and reburied Ramses in the tomb of his father, Seti I. Later, under the high priest of Amun Pinedjem II in Dynasty Twenty-one, the mummies of Ramses II, his father, and a number of other pharaohs were all transferred to a tomb in the cliffs at Deir el-Bahari near the mortuary temple of Queen Hatshepsut. There the mummies remained until they were discovered by the Department of Antiquities in 1881 and taken to Cairo.

The coffin is made of bare wood. The king's insignia (crook, flail, beard, and uraeus) were made separately and then attached to the coffin. In addition, some details have been painted: eyes, hair, chin straps, and bracelets. The coffin may have been carved some time near the end of the Eighteenth Dynasty, but the insignia seem to have been added in the Twenty-first Dynasty at the time of Ramses' reburial.

On the abdomen and thighs is a hieratic inscription in black ink documenting the king's rewrapping and reburial. This inscription explains how the mummy of Ramses was removed from the tomb of Seti I. Above are the cartouches of Ramses II, added by the ancient scribe to identify the mummy.

Cairo Museum entry no.: 26214.
Museum catalog no.: 61020.
Height: 2.06 m. Maximum width: 54.5 cm.
Depth of feet: 36.5 cm.
Provenance: Thebes.
Date: Coffin, New Kingdom.
Reburials, Late Dynasty 20 and Third Intermediate Period.

When a body was mummified, the viscera were removed and mummified separately in four containers called canopic jars. At first the stoppers of these jars were carved in the likeness of human heads. In later dynasties they were carved in the likeness of the funerary deities known as the four sons of Horus. The stoppers of royal canopic jars, however, were carved in the likeness of the deceased.

This canopic jar stopper, discovered in Tomb 80 in the Valley of the Queens in Thebes, portrays Queen Tuya, wife of Seti I and mother of Ramses II. The eyes and eyebrows of the calcite head were once inlaid with colored glass, and other parts of the head were colorfully decorated. A broad collar necklace composed of many rows of beads is around her neck.

The queen wears an elaborate heavy wig, partly covered by a vulture cap. The wings of the vulture frame the queen's face, and the vulture's head, now broken, once extended over her forehead. Known from the time of the Old Kingdom, the vulture cap identified the queen as the king's mother.

Luxor Museum entry no.: J.191.
Height: 17 cm.
Maximum diameter of head: 15 cm.
Provenance: Thebes.
Date: New Kingdom, Dynasty 19.

This short faience tube held kohl, an Egyptian eye makeup. Kohl is made of powdered galena, a dark grey lead ore, mixed with a gum substance and water, and then dried. The kohl was applied to the eyes with a wood, ivory, or bronze applicator called a kohl stick. This container has been made into a decorative piece with the addition of a squatting monkey to hold and present the tube. The monkey was popular with the ancient Egyptians as a household pet, and toilet articles and vessels were commonly decorated with its likeness.

The two holes on either side of the top of the tube were used to fasten down the lid. The figure of the monkey was painted with black spots before the piece was fired.

Cairo Museum entry no.: 31244.
Museum catalog no.: 3979.
Height: 5 cm.
Provenance: Kaw (?).
Date: New Kingdom.

Molded in blue faience, this double-tubed kohl container held two colors of eye makeup. (Some kohl containers are known to have as many as six tubes.) The two most commonly used colors were green, made from the copper ore malachite, and black, made from galena.

This case is decorated in black paint with a frieze of small hanging lotus flowers at the top and a frieze of hanging lotus petals at the bottom. In the center a woman is sketched, indicating that this is an object for female use. She has one arm bent across her chest, and the other is at her side holding a lotus bud. Tubes made of other materials, such as ivory, exhibit the female figure carved in relief.

There is a small hole between the two kohl tubes to hold the applicator.

Cairo Museum entry no.: 72178.
Museum catalog no.: 3978.
Height: 13 cm.
Provenance: Abydos.
Date: New Kingdom.

This kohl pot is in the traditional New Kingdom shape, with a concave profile below the rim. The most common material used to make kohl pots was alabaster, but often they were made of faience, as was this one.

Faience is a ware made from glazed quartz frit. These vessels were shaped in a mold, formed on a wheel, or built up by hand. They were then decorated and fired. The firing hardened the vessel and produced its lustrous blue finish.

This kohl vessel was probably shaped on a wheel, and before firing it was painted with black-dotted lotus petals. A flat decorated lid covers its cylindrical opening. A small amount of kohl still remains inside.

Cairo Museum entry no.: 30776.
Museum catalog no.: 3681.
Height: 4.7 cm. Width: 3.8 cm.
Provenance: Abydos.
Date: New Kingdom.

Found in Gurna on the West Bank of Thebes, this miniature box is made of wood inlaid with ivory. The knob on the removable lid serves as a handle, as well as a way to seal the box. A string could be tied around this knob and the one on the side and "sealed" with a lump of clay stamped with the name of the owner. Judging from its small size, this box probably held jewelry.

The shape of the box imitates the design of the Palace of the South, residence of the prehistoric kings of Upper Egypt. This structure was characterized by a roof that bulged up and then curved back. Shrines of this type would have displayed a protective winged disc on the bulge of the roof. In place of the disc, the box displays vertical lines of ivory. The Palace of the South also had an extended edge under the roof with a decorated cavetto cornice below. This box shows both of those elements.

Cairo Museum entry no.: 3318.
Height: 7.8 cm.
Provenance: Thebes.
Date: New Kingdom.

This small schist dish is carved in the shape of the bulti fish, *Tilapia nilotica* (see also object 6). One of the most common Nile fishes, the bulti was called both *inet* and *wajd* by the ancient Egyptians. *Wajd* means "fresh" or "green," and, in an extended sense, "eternally young." Thus this fish came to be a common symbol of rebirth or resurrection.

Perhaps the dish's owner believed the *wajd* shape would keep perfume or oil magically fresh. This type of dish may also have been placed in the tomb to hold an ointment needed for the resurrection of the deceased.

Cairo Museum entry no.: 25226.
Museum catalog no.: 18551.
Length: 11.4 cm. Width: 5.8 cm.
Provenance: Purchased.
Date: New Kingdom.

This decorative wooden ladle was used to hold an unguent or some kind of perfumed grease. The ladle consists of a rounded receptacle, or bowl, with a rather broad, flat handle. Around the edge of the bowl are decorative zigzag lines representing water, and two lotuses form corners at the end.

The carved handle depicts a swamp scene. Two men pole a papyrus skiff across water, again represented by zigzag lines. Tall papyrus stalks, alternating with buds and flowers, form the background. A young calf lies in the skiff.

If the ladle is stood on end, the bowl becomes the sun, rising over or out of the marsh.

Cairo Museum entry no.: 49540.
Height: 21.5 cm. Bowl diameter: 9 cm.
Provenance: Sakkara.
Date: Late Period (?).

A young woman standing in the midst of hollyhocks is painted on this glazed tile fragment. The woman, with long black hair that is now mostly broken away, wears earrings and bracelets. Curving over her head is a lotus flower.

The woman has a stick in her hand, but what she is doing with it remains unclear. A similar tile fragment in the Metropolitan Museum in New York, also from the Ramesside Palace at Qantir, would suggest the woman is nude.

The hollyhock is one of several plants brought to Egypt from Syria in the early Eighteenth Dynasty.

Cairo Museum entry no.: 89483.
Height: 18.9 cm. Width: 18.4 cm.
Provenance: Qantir.
Date: New Kingdom, Dynasty 19.

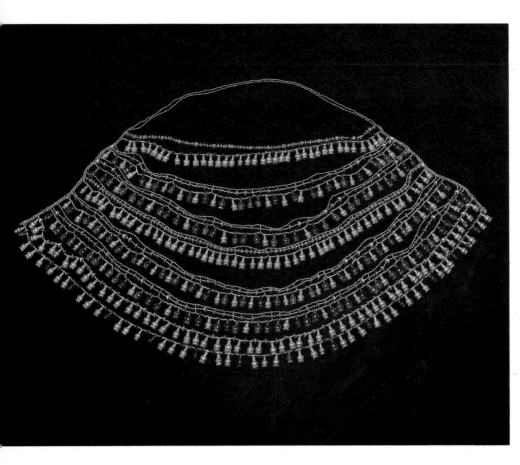

In 1906 and 1907 two hoards of ancient treasure were found at the city of Zagazig, ancient Bubastis, in the Delta. From one of these finds came the exquisite gold and carnelian beads used to reconstruct this necklace (see also objects 49, 51, and 67). The necklace is composed of nineteen rows of beads with spacers. The first two rows, as well as the last two, are single strings of beads, but all the rest of the necklace is composed of triple strings of beads.

The smallest of the beads are gold; the slightly larger oval ones are a gold alloy. The drop beads, resembling hanging cornflowers, are gold and carnelian.

Cairo Museum entry no.: 39875.
Museum catalog no.: 53184.
Width of present mounting: 36 cm.
Provenance: Bubastis.
Date: New Kingdom, Dynasty 19 (?).

Metal mirrors appeared in ancient Egypt as early as the Old Kingdom. Although Ptolemaic temple reliefs sometimes show a gold mirror symbolizing the sun and a silver one the moon, mirror discs were usually made of bronze. Their polished surfaces were protected by wood or leather cases.

Both the disc and handle of this mirror are bronze, but handles were also commonly made from wood or ivory. The most popular handle shape was a papyrus stalk, which represented beauty and freshness. The handle on this mirror, however, is in the shape of a nude woman standing on a small square base. On her head is a heavy wig that supports the calyx of the papyrus flower into which the disc is riveted.

Cairo Museum entry no.: 10888.
Museum catalog no.: 44044.
Height: 30.5 cm.
Provenance: Sakkara.
Date: New Kingdom.

This painted limestone statue of a queen, broken away at the waist, was found in a small chapel just northwest of the walls of the Ramesseum. It now seems certain this statue is of Meryet-amun, daughter of Ramses II and Nefertari, for another was recently found at Akhmin carrying the same titles as those found on the back of this piece. Because of the white limestone apparent in her face and body, this statue is often referred to as the "White Queen."

The queen's status is shown by the *modius* encircled with uraei and discs on top of her head and the pair of crowned uraei attached to the front of the diadem around her wig. In her left hand she holds the necklace with counterweight, called the *menat*, which is a symbol of the goddess Hathor. Women involved in the cult of Hathor were generally concerned with ritual singing, dancing, and music playing. The fragmentary inscription on the back of the statue gives part of her titles as "Sistrum Player for the Goddess Mut" and "Ritual Dancer for the God Horus."

The queen wears a long tripartite wig that falls down her back and over both shoulders; a headband across her forehead holds her own hair. A broad collar of six rows of beads encircles her neck. The top five are in the shape of the hieroglyphic sign *nefer*, "beauty." A moderate amount of yellow and blue paint still remains on the piece.

Cairo Museum entry no.: 31413.
Museum catalog no.: 600.
Height: 75 cm. Width: 44 cm.
Provenance: Thebes.
Date: New Kingdom, Dynasty 19.

This small chalice was fashioned for Queen Tawosret, the last ruler of the Nineteenth Dynasty. Her name appears in a cartouche on the stem, surmounted by the feathers and disc similar to those on the queen's crown.

The cup and stem were made separately from gold sheeting and then soldered together. The cup portrays a blossom of the white lotus, and the pronounced veins in the outer petals are characteristic of this variety. The stem, on the other hand, resembles a papyrus stalk with flower, placed upside down.

Representations of royalty drinking from a white-lotus chalice are known from the later Eighteenth Dynasty on. It may well be that this was the typical form of royal drinking vessels.

This cup was part of a hoard found at Bubastis, modern Zagazig, in the Delta (see also objects 49, 51, and 64).

Cairo Museum entry no.: 39872.
Museum catalog no.: 53260.
Height: 9.5 cm. Cup diameter: 8 cm.
Base diameter: 4.3 cm.
Provenance: Bubastis.
Date: New Kingdom, Dynasty 19.

This flat wooden comb has evenly shaped and spaced teeth that end in a straight edge. Only the two outermost teeth are thicker to prevent breakage. This is the most common shape of the New Kingdom comb, and many like this have been found.

The comb's handle is carved with four evenly spaced tangs and a stylized band of lotus petals.

Wooden combs were the most common in ancient Egypt, although ivory combs have also been found.

Cairo Museum entry no.: 36233.
Museum catalog no.: 44316.
Height: 5 cm. Length: 17 cm.
Provenance: Abusir el-Malik.
Date: New Kingdom.

This swan-shaped bowl is made of alabaster. The upper part of the swan's body forms the oval bowl, and the swan's turned neck and head serve as the handle. The variegations in the alabaster resemble the markings of the bird's plumage. There are frequent examples of this type of container in the shape of a duck, but swan-shaped bowls are rare.

The swan appeared in ancient Egypt as a migratory bird, but it was not common and seems not to have played any particular role in Egyptian folklore or mythology. Scholars are not even sure of the ancient Egyptian name for swan.

Cairo Museum entry no.: 30759.
Museum catalog no.: 18566.
Length: 14.3 cm.
Provenance: Sakkara.
Date: New Kingdom.

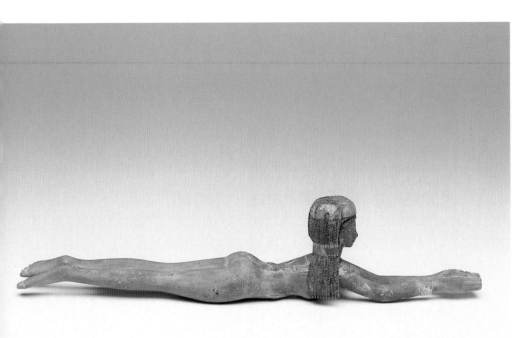

This wooden spoon handle has been carved in the shape of a nude swimming girl. A circular container, probably duck shaped with wings for a lid, was attached to the top of her hands. This particular type of decorative handle was most common in the later Eighteenth Dynasty.

Gold traces left on the wood show where a girdle once went around the hips of the figure and straps crossed over her back. She also wears bracelets, and a broad bead collar is carved around her neck. Her elaborate hair is held back in a large lock that falls down her right side. A wide headband, originally decorated with flowers, encircles her head.

The container once held by this handle was probably for cosmetics used in the home. If there was a ritual interpretation for the figure of a girl pulled by a duck, the spoon's bowl likely held a substance applied during burial rites.

Cairo Museum entry no.: 5218.
Museum catalog no.: 45118.
Length: 34.5 cm.
Provenance: Purchased.
Date: New Kingdom, Late Dynasty 18.

Ramesside monuments text, C. Wilfred Griggs

This 65–foot statue is one of four guarding the temple of Ramses II at Abu Simbel. Two statues are seated on each side of the temple's entrance, and they undoubtedly impressed northbound travelers that this temple marked the gateway to a great and powerful land ruled by a heroic and divine king. Ramses' statue was also carved in the shrine of the temple, some 160 feet into the mountain. Twice a year the rising sun shone back into the shrine, illuminating the pharaoh's image and also that of the god of Thebes, Amun Re.

This magnificent temple, hewn into the rock cliffs near the Nile River on Egypt's southern border, reminded southbound Egyptian travelers of their land's grandeur. Nubians and other Egyptianized southerners were encouraged to continue in peace with a powerful leader who could marshall the resources to build such spectacular edifices. To further awe the travelers, tales of military triumph were carved on the inner walls of the temple (some of the earliest known propaganda in the world).

The temple of Hathor, the northern temple of Abu Simbel, was built by Ramses II to honor his favorite wife, Queen Nefertari. Between the statues of Ramses are those of Nefertari, and the size of her statues signifies that she will be honored to nearly the same degree as her husband in her relationship to the gods. Both temples at Abu Simbel were used as storehouses for treasures and tribute exacted from Nubia, thus combining the temples' essentially religious function with an eminently practical one.

Two of the most famous pharaohs of Egypt, Amenophis III and Ramses II, are responsible for enlarging and completing the Temple of Luxor, constructed on a site considered holy from ancient times. The earlier pharaoh enlarged the structure, and Ramses II later added a colonnaded court and two obelisks in front of the temple. (One remains, but the other is in Paris, a gift to France in honor of Champollion's decipherment of Egyptian hieroglyphs.) Ramses also erected six colossal statues, of which only four remain, two seated and two standing.

Even when Ramses did not originally construct a monument, he often usurped it for himself by erecting his own statuary and redecorating the walls with his cartouches and stories of his exploits.

C. Wilfred Griggs

Begun well before the time of Ramses II, the Karnak temple complex grew to become one of the largest sacred sites in the world, encompassing more than 250 acres. In this already stupendous setting, the most celebrated and spectacular part of the Karnak Temple is the hypostyle hall between the second and third pylons (gates).

Ramses completed this hall in grand fashion, and it is a veritable forest of columns—122 of them. The tallest are approximately 75 feet high, and many are decorated with the deeply incised hieroglyphs that have become a trademark of Ramses II.

One of the seven wonders of the ancient world, the Giza pyramids still inspire awe in the modern visitor. The largest of the three, that of Cheops or Khufu, stands approximately 470 feet high and measures some 750 feet along each side. It contains over 2½ million stone blocks, some weighing up to 15 tons.

The pyramids, together with the ancient temple complexes associated with them, were majestic witnesses through the succeeding centuries of the religious beliefs of their Egyptian builders. As homes for the dead, they were also passages to eternity, symbolized in part by their shape's resemblance to the sun's rays and their orientation to the cardinal directions.

One can better appreciate the age of the pyramids by remembering they were well over 1,000 years old by the time Ramses II began to reign.

"Egypt is an acquired country, the gift of the Nile." In this famous quotation, Herodotus epitomizes how the whole of Egyptian civilization ultimately turns back to the river. The annual flooding with its promise of regeneration to the land, the seasons of the year that correspond with the river's flow, and travel downstream with the current and upstream with the wind—all are reminders of the Nile's impact upon Egyptian life.

For countless sunrises and sunsets the dwellers in this great river valley have influenced other cultures throughout the world. Even now the influence of Ramses II continues to stretch across the centuries through the cultural exhibit that bears his name.

1. Porter and Moss, *Topographical Bibliography* V, p. 226.
Desroches-Noblecourt, *Ramses Le Grand*, pp. 56–57.
Desroches-Noblecourt, *The Great Pharaoh*, no. 3.

2. Desroches-Noblecourt, *The Great Pharaoh*, no. 9.

3. Terrace and Fischer, *Treasures of Egyptian Art*, pp. 149–52.
Smith, *Art and Architecture*, pp. 235–36 and pl. 170A.
Desroches-Noblecourt, *Ramses Le Grand*, pp. 134–35.
Desroches-Noblecourt, *The Great Pharaoh*, no. 15.

4. Legrain, *Statues* II, p. 29 and pl. XXVI.
Aldred, *Egyptian Art*, p. 202, fig. 167.
Desroches-Noblecourt, *Ramses Le Grand*, pp. 136–37.
Desroches-Noblecourt, *The Great Pharaoh*, no. 7.

5. Desroches-Noblecourt, *Ramses Le Grand*, pp. 277–79.
Desroches-Noblecourt, *The Great Pharaoh*, no. 19.

6. Desroches-Noblecourt, *Ramses Le Grand*, pp. 277–79.
Desroches-Noblecourt, *The Great Pharaoh*, no. 18.

7. Montet and Bucher, *Revue Biblique* 44 (1935): 153–65, and pls. V–VI.
Montet, *Egypt and the Bible*, p. 23, pl. II.
Vandier, *Manuel* III, pl. CXXXIII, no. 2.
Desroches-Noblecourt, *Ramses Le Grand*, pp. 5–11.
Desroches-Noblecourt, *The Great Pharaoh*, no. 4.

8. Legrain, *Statues* II, pp. 32–33 and pl. XXIX.
Vandier, *Manuel* III, pl. CLXXIV, no. 6.
Desroches-Noblecourt, *The Great Pharaoh*, unnumbered.

9. Desroches-Noblecourt, *Ramses Le Grand*, pp. 111–13.
Desroches-Noblecourt, *The Great Pharaoh*, no. 10.

10. Desroches-Noblecourt, *Ramses Le Grand*, p. 282.
Desroches-Noblecourt, *The Great Pharaoh*, no. 22.

11. Desroches-Noblecourt, *Ramses Le Grand*, pp. 277–79.
Desroches-Noblecourt, *The Great Pharaoh*, no. 17.

12. Montet, *Psousennès*, pp. 97–98 and pl. LXV.
Desroches-Noblecourt, *Ramses Le Grand*, pp. 294–95.
Desroches-Noblecourt, *The Great Pharaoh*, no. 25.

13. Porter and Moss, *Topographical Bibliography* I, part 2, p. 509.
Desroches-Noblecourt, *The Great Pharaoh*, no. 44.

14. Montet, *Psousennès*, pp. 99–100 and pls. LXVII-LXVIII.
Smith, *Art and Architecture*, p. 234 and pl. 169A.
Desroches-Noblecourt, *Ramses Le Grand*, pp. 308–309.
Desroches-Noblecourt, *The Great Pharaoh*, no. 30.

15. Montet, *Psousennès*, p. 100, fig. 42, and pl. LXVIII.
Desroches-Noblecourt, *Ramses Le Grand*, pp. 308–309.
Desroches-Noblecourt, *The Great Pharaoh*, no. 31.

16. Sloley, *Ancient Egypt* (1924) pp. 43–50.
Parker, *Calendars*, p. 40.
Desroches-Noblecourt, *Ramses Le Grand*, pp. 139–49.
Desroches-Noblecourt, *The Great Pharaoh*, no. 8.

17. Daressy, *Annales du Service des Antiquités de L'Égypte* 11 (1911): 3 and pl IIb
Hayes, *Glazed Tiles*, pp. 31–32 and fig. 9.
Desroches-Noblecourt, *Ramses Le Grand*, pp. 280–81.
Desroches-Noblecourt, *The Great Pharaoh*, no. 21.

18. Montet, *Psousennès*, pp. 96–97 and pl. LXV.
Desroches-Noblecourt, *Ramses Le Grand*, pp. 304–305.
Desroches-Noblecourt, *The Great Pharaoh*, no. 29.

19. Legrain, *Statues* II, pp. 11–12 and pl. VIII.
Desroches-Noblecourt, *Ramses Le Grand*, pp. 238–41.
Desroches-Noblecourt, *The Great Pharaoh*, no. 65.

20. Legrain, *Statues* II, pp. 7–8 and pl. IV.
Desroches-Noblecourt, *Ramses Le Grand*, pp. 232–37.
Desroches-Noblecourt, *The Great Pharaoh*, no. 64.

21. Desroches-Noblecourt, *The Great Pharaoh*, no. 47.

22. Desroches-Noblecourt, *The Great Pharaoh*, no. 50.

23. Bruyère, *La Tombe de Sen-nedjem*, pp. 52–53 and pl. XVII.
Porter and Moss, *Topographical Bibliography* I, part I, p. 3.
Koenigsberger, *Die Konstruktion der Ägyptischen Tür*, p. 17, fig. 16.
Desroches-Noblecourt, *Ramses Le Grand*, pp. 189–93.
Desroches-Noblecourt, *The Great Pharaoh*, no. 45.

24. Porter and Moss, *Topographical Bibliography* I, part I, p. 5.

Desroches-Noblecourt, *Ramses Le Grand*, pp. 194–205.

Desroches-Noblecourt, *The Great Pharaoh*, no. 48.

25. Porter and Moss, *Topographical Bibliography* I, part I, p. 4.

Desroches-Noblecourt, *Ramses Le Grand*, pp. 165–67.

Desroches-Noblecourt, *The Great Pharaoh*, no. 33.

26. Porter and Moss, *Topographical Bibliography* I, part I, p. 4.

Desroches-Noblecourt, *Ramses Le Grand*, pp. 168–69.

Desroches-Noblecourt, *The Great Pharaoh*, no. 34.

27. Porter and Moss, *Topographical Bibliography* I, part I, p. 5.

Desroches-Noblecourt, *Ramses Le Grand*, pp. 170–71.

Desroches-Noblecourt, *The Great Pharaoh*, no. 35.

28. Desroches-Noblecourt, *Ramses Le Grand*, pp. 172–73.

Desroches-Noblecourt, *The Great Pharaoh*, no. 36.

29. Newberry, *Funerary Statuettes* III, pl. XXIII.

Ĉerný, *Community of Workmen*, p. 117, nn. 5 and 8.

Desroches-Noblecourt, *The Great Pharaoh*, no. 51.

30. Newberry, *Funerary Statuettes* III, pl. XXIV.

Desroches-Noblecourt, *The Great Pharaoh*, no. 52.

31. Bruyère, *Fouilles de Deir el Médineh*, 1924–1925, p. 15 and fig. 9.

Egypt's Golden Age, pp. 65–66, and fig. 28.

Desroches-Noblecourt, *Ramses Le Grand*, pp. 186–88.

Desroches-Noblecourt, *The Great Pharaoh*, no. 39.

32. Eggebrecht, in *Das Alte Agypten*, p. 358 and pl. XLVIIb.

Desroches-Noblecourt, *The Great Pharaoh*, no. 42.

33. Toda, *Annales du Service des Antiquités de L'Égypte* 20 (1920): 154.

Porter and Moss, *Topographical Bibliography* I, part I, p. 4.

34. Desroches-Noblecourt, *The Great Pharaoh*, no. 43.

35. Capart, *Chronique D'Égypte* 32 (1941): 200–201 and fig. 5.

Desroches-Noblecourt, *Ramses Le Grand*, pp. 174–75.

Desroches-Noblecourt, *The Great Pharaoh*, no. 37.

36. Desroches-Noblecourt, *The Great Pharaoh*, no. 49.

37. Porter and Moss, *Topographical Bibliography* I, part I, p. 4.

Desroches-Noblecourt, *Ramses Le Grand*, p. 176.

Desroches-Noblecourt, *The Great Pharaoh*, no. 38.

38. Desroches-Noblecourt, *Ramses Le Grand*, pp. 68–71.

Desroches-Noblecourt, *The Great Pharaoh*, no. 6.

39. Desroches-Noblecourt, *The Great Pharaoh*, no. 41.

40. Desroches-Noblecourt, *The Great Pharaoh*, no. 40.

41. Desroches-Noblecourt, *The Great Pharaoh*, no. 54.

42. Desroches-Noblecourt, *Ramses Le Grand*, pp. 130–31.

Kischkewitz and Forman, *Egyptian Drawings*, no. 9.

Desroches-Noblecourt, *The Great Pharaoh*, no. 13.

43. Vandier d'Abbadie, *Ostraca figurés*, p. 158 and pl. XCIV.

Desroches-Noblecourt, *Ramses Le Grand*, pp. 132–33.

Desroches-Noblecourt, *The Great Pharaoh*, no. 14.

44. Hickmann, *Instruments de Musique*, p. 7 and pl. IIa.

Desroches-Noblecourt, *The Great Pharaoh*, no. 12.

46. Foucart, *Bulletin de L'Institut Français D'Archéologie Orientale* 24 (1924): 103 and pl. XI.

Bruyère, *Fouilles de Deir el-Médineh*, 1935–1940, p. 7 and fig. 76.

Desroches-Noblecourt, *Ramses Le Grand*, pp. 124–27.

Desroches-Noblecourt, *The Great Pharaoh*, no. 11.

47. Maspero, *Zeitschrift für Ägyptische Sprache und Alterumskunde* 48 (1910): 91–96.

Roeder, *Naos* p. 22 and pl. 6.

Desroches-Noblecourt, *Ramses Le Grand*, pp. 151–60.

Desroches-Noblecourt, *The Great Pharaoh*, no. 2.

48. Montet, *Psousennès*, pp. 136–37 and pl. CVIII.

Wilkinson, *Ancient Egyptian Jewellery*, pp. 173–74 and pl. LXIII.

Desroches-Noblecourt, *Ramses Le Grand*, pp. 306–307.

Desroches-Noblecourt, *The Great Pharaoh*, no. 32.

49. Vernier, *Bijoux et Orfèvreries*, pp.183–84, pl. XVIII.
Aldred, *Jewels of the Pharaohs*, fig. 129 and pp. 232–33.
Wilkinson, *Ancient Egyptian Jewellery*, p. 151 and pl. LVII.
Desroches-Noblecourt, *Ramses Le Grand*, pp. 299–301.
Desroches-Noblecourt, *The Great Pharaoh*, no. 23.

50. Desroches-Noblecourt, *Ramses Le Grand*, pp. 64–67.
Kitchen, *Ramesside Inscriptions* II, p. 711.
Desroches-Noblecourt, *The Great Pharaoh*, no. 1.

51. Vernier, *Bijoux et Orfèvreries*, pp. 416–17 and pl. CV.
Edgar, *Annales du Service des Antiquités de L'Égypte* 25 (1925): 256–58 and pls. I-II.
Desroches-Noblecourt, *Ramses Le Grand*, p. 288–93.
Desroches-Noblecourt, *The Great Pharaoh*, no. 16.

52. Winlock, *Journal of Egyptian Archaeology* 10 (1924): 258.
Porter and Moss, *Topographical Bibliography* I, part II, p. 605.
Pusch, *Das Senet-Brettspiel*, p. 195 and pl. 45.
Desroches-Noblecourt, *The Great Pharaoh*, no. 46.

53. Vernier, *Bijoux et Orfèvreries*, pp. 137–38 and pl. XXVIII.
Aldred, *Jewels of the Pharaohs*, fig. 130 and pp. 233–34.
Wilkinson, *Ancient Egyptian Jewellery*, p. 155 and pl. LXA.
Desroches-Noblecourt, *Ramses Le Grand*, pp. 302–303.
Desroches-Noblecourt, *The Great Pharaoh*, no. 24.

54. Terrace and Fischer, *Treasures of Egyptian Art*, pp. 141–44.
Aldred, *Jewels of the Pharaohs*, p. 243, and fig. 150.
Desroches-Noblecourt, *Ramses Le Grand*, pp. 84–85.
Desroches-Noblecourt, *The Great Pharaoh*, no. 67.

55. Maspero, *Momies Royales*, pp. 556–60.
Daressy, *Cercueils des Cachettes Royales*, pp. 32–34 and pls. XX–XXII.
Thomas, *The Royal Necropoleis*, pp. 252–53.
Kitchen, *Third Intermediate Period*, pp. 252, 277–78, 417, and 423.
Desroches-Noblecourt, *Ramses Le Grand*, pp. 316–22.
Desroches-Noblecourt, *The Great Pharaoh*, no. 67.

56. Desroches-Noblecourt, *Ramses Le Grand*, pp. 28–31.
Luxor Museum, *Catalogue*, p. 142.
Desroches-Noblecourt, *The Great Pharaoh*, no. 5.

57. von Bissing, *Fayencegefässe*, p. 86.
Desroches-Noblecourt, *The Great Pharaoh*, no. 62.

58. von Bissing, *Fayencegefässe*, pp. 85–86.
Desroches-Noblecourt, *The Great Pharaoh*, no. 63.

59. Bénédite, *Objects de Toilette* I, p. 54 and pl. XXII.
von Bissing, *Fayencegefässe*, pp. 23–24.
Desroches-Noblecourt, *The Great Pharaoh*, no. 61.

60. Desroches-Noblecourt, *The Great Pharaoh*, no. 56.

61. von Bissing, *Steingefässe*, pp. 112–13.
Desroches-Noblecourt, *The Great Pharaoh*, no. 57.

62. Wallert, *Der Verzierte Löffel*, p. 103.
Desroches-Noblecourt, *The Great Pharaoh*, no. 59.

63. Hayes, *Glazed Tiles*, pp. 39–40 and pl. XII.
Desroches-Noblecourt, *Ramses Le Grand*, pp. 277–79.
Desroches-Noblecourt, *The Great Pharaoh*, no. 20.

64. Vernier, *Bijoux et Orfèvreries*, p. 388 and pl. LXXXIII.
Wilkinson, *Ancient Egyptian Jewellery*, p. 50 and pl. LVIIIB.
Desroches-Noblecourt, *Ramses Le Grand*, p. 298.
Desroches-Noblecourt, *The Great Pharaoh*, no. 27.

65. Bénédite, *Miroirs*, p. 23 and pl. XI.
Desroches-Noblecourt, *The Great Pharaoh*, no. 53.

66. Petrie, *Six Temples*, pp. 6–7 and pl. XXIII.
Borchardt, *Statuen*, p. 152.
Lange and Hirmer, *Egypt*, pl. LIV and p. 502.
Yoyotte, *Treasures of the Pharaoh*, p. 145.
Desroches-Noblecourt, *Ramses Le Grand*, pp. 72–74.
Desroches-Noblecourt, *The Great Pharaoh*, no. 28.

67. Vernier, *Bijoux et Orfèvreries*, p. 415 and pl. CIV.
Desroches-Noblecourt, *Ramses Le Grand*, pp. 296–297.
Desroches-Noblecourt, *The Great Pharaoh*, no. 26.

68. Bénédite, *Objects de Toilette* I, pp. 6–7 and pl. IV.
Desroches-Noblecourt, *The Great Pharaoh*, no. 55.

69. von Bissing, *Steingefässe*, p. 116 and pl. VIII.
Vandier D'Abbadie, *Revue D'Egyptologie* 25 (1973): 45 and pl. 3.
Desroches-Noblecourt, *The Great Pharaoh*, no. 58.

70. Bénédite, *Objects de Toilette* II, pls. 28 and 31.
Wallert, *Der Verzierte Löffel*, p. 95.
Jordan, *Egypt the Black Land*, p. 167.
Desroches-Noblecourt, *The Great Pharaoh*, no. 60.

Aldred, C. *Egyptian Art*. London: Thames and Hudson, 1980.

_____. *Jewels of the Pharaohs*. New York: Praeger Publishers, 1971.

Bénédite, G. *Miroirs, Catalogue Général des Antiquités Égyptiennes*. Cairo, 1907.

_____. *Objects des Toilette* I, *Catalogue Général des Antiquités Égyptiennes*. Cairo, 1911.

Borchardt, L. *Statuen und Stauetten von Königen und Privatleuten* II, *Catalogue Général des Antiquités Égyptiennes*. Berlin, 1925.

Bruyère, B. *Rapport sur les Fouilles de Deir el-Médineh, 1924–1925*. Cairo: French Institute, 1926.

_____. *Rapport sur les Fouilles de Deir el-Médineh, 1935–1940*. Cairo: French Institute, 1952.

_____. *La Tombe No. 1 de Sen-nedjem*. Cairo: French Institute, 1959.

Capart, J. "Statuettes Funéraires Égyptiennes." *Chronique D'Égypte* 43 (1941): 196–204.

Černý, J. *A Community of Workmen at Thebes in the Ramesside Period*. Cairo: French Institute, 1973.

Daressy, G. *Cercueils des Cachettes Royales, Catalogue Général des Antiquités Égyptiennes*. Cairo, 1909.

_____. "Note sur l'article précédent." *Annales du Service des Antiquités de L'Égypte* 20 (1920): 159–60.

_____. "Plaquettes Émaillées de Médinet-Habou." *Annales du Service des Antiquités de L'Égypte* 11 (1911): 49–63.

Desroches-Noblecourt, C. *The Great Pharaoh Ramses II and His Time*. Exhibition catalogue. Montréal, 1985.

Desroches-Noblecourt, C., et al. *Ramses Le Grand*. Exhibition catalogue. Paris, 1976.

Edgar, C. C. "Engraved Designs on a Silver Vase from Tell Basta." *Annales du Service des Antiquités de L'Égypte* 25 (1925):256–58.

Eggebrecht, A. *In* Vandersleyen, *Das Alte Ägypten*. Berlin: Propyläen Kunstgeschichte, 1975.

Egypt's Golden Age: The Art of Living in the New Kingdom. Exhibition catalogue. Boston: Museum of Fine Arts, 1982.

Foucart, G. "La Belle Fête de la Vallée." *Bulletin de L'Institut Français D'Archéologie Orientale* 24 (1924): 1–148.

Hayes, W. C. *Glazed Tiles from a Palace of Ramesses II at Kantir*. New York: Metropolitan Museum of Art, 1937.

Hickmann, H. *Instruments de Musique, Catalogue Général des Antiquités Égyptiennes*. Cairo, 1949.

Jordan, P. *Egypt the Black Land*. Oxford: Phaidon Press, 1976.

Kischkewitz, H., and W. Forman. *Egyptian Drawings*. London: Octopus Books, 1972.

Kitchen, K. A. *Ramesside Inscriptions* II. Oxford: B. H. Blackwell, 1979.

_____. *The Third Intermediate Period in Egypt*. Warminster: Aris and Phillips, 1973.

Koenigsberger, O. *Die Konstruktion der Ägyptischen Tür, Ägyptologische Forschungen*. Glückstadt, 1936.

Lange, K., and M. Hirmer. *Egypt*. New York: Phaidon Press, 1968.

Legrain, G. *Statues et Statuettes de Rois et de Particuliers, Catalogue Général des Antiquités Égyptiennes*. Cairo, 1909.

Luxor Museum of Ancient Art. *Catalogue*. Cairo: American Research Center in Egypt, 1979.

Maspero, G. "La Chapelle Nouvelle d'Ibsamboul." *Zeitschrift für Ägyptische Sprache und Alterumskunde* 48 (1910): 91–96.

_____. *Les Momies Royales de Deir el-Bahari*. Paris: Ernest Leroux, 1889.

Montet, P. *Egypt and the Bible*. Philadelphia: Fortress Press, 1968.

_____. *Les Constructions et le Tombeau de Psousennès a Tanis, La Nécropole Royale de Tanis* II. Paris, 1951.

Montet, P., and P. Bucher. "Un Dieu Cananéen a Tanis Houroun de Ramsès." *Revue Biblique* 44 (1935): 153–65.

Newberry, P. *Funerary Statuettes and Model Sarcophagi, Catalogue Général des Antiquités Égyptiennes*. Cairo, 1957.

Parker, R. A. *The Calendars of Ancient Egypt, Studies in Ancient Oriental Civilization* 26. 1950.

Petrie, W. M. F. *Six Temples at Thebes*. London, 1897.

Porter, B., and R. L. B. Moss. *Topographical Bibliography of Ancient Egyptian Hieroglyphic Texts, Reliefs and Paintings* I, parts I and II. 2d ed. Oxford: Griffith Institute, 1970 and 1973.

_____. *Topographical Bibliography of Ancient Egyptian Hieroglyphic Texts, Reliefs and Paintings* V. Oxford: Clarendon Press, 1937.

Pusch, E. B. *Das Senet-Brettspiel im Alten Ägypten, Münchner Ägyptologische Studien* 38. 1979.

Roeder, G. *Naos, Catalogue Général des Antiquités Égyptiennes*. Leipzig, 1914.

Sloley, R. W. "Ancient Clepsydrae." *Ancient Egypt* (1924): 43–50.

Smith, W. S. *Art and Architecture of Ancient Egypt*. Baltimore, Maryland: Penguin Books, 1965.

Terrace, E. L. B., and H. G. Fischer. *Treasures of Egyptian Art from the Cairo Museum*. Boston: Museum of Fine Arts, 1970.

Thomas, E. *The Royal Necropoleis of Thebes*. Princeton, 1966.

Toda, E. "La Découverte et L'Inventaire du Tombeau de Sennezem." *Annales du Service des Antiquités de L'Égypte* 20 (1920): 145–59.

Vandier D'Abbadie, J. "Le Cygne dans L'Égypte Ancienne." *Revue D'Égyptologie* 25 (1973): 35–49.

_____. *Ostraca figurés de Deir el-Medineh* III. Cairo: French Institute, 1946.

Vandier, J. *Manuel D'Archéologie Égyptienne* III, *La Statuaire*. Paris: A. and J. Picard, 1958.

Vernier, E. *Bijoux et Orfèvreries, Catalogue Général des Antiquités Égyptiennes*. Cairo, 1927.

von Bissing, F. W. *Fayencegefässe, Catalogue Général des Antiquités Égyptiennes*. Vienna, 1902.

_____. *Steingefässe, Catalogue Général des Antiquités Égyptiennes*. Vienna, 1907.

Wallert, I. *Der Verzierte Löffel, Ägyptologische Abhandlung* 16. Wiesbaden, 1967.

Wilkinson, A. *Ancient Egyptian Jewellery*. London: Methuen and Co., 1971.

Winlock, H. E. "The Tombs of the Kings of the Seventeenth Dynasty at Thebes." *Journal of Egyptian Archaeology* 10 (1924): 217–77.

Yoyotte, J. *Treasures of the Pharaohs*. Geneva: Skira, 1968.

Printing: BYU Print Services
Typography: Jonathan Skousen,
Provo, Utah
Color Separations: International
Color, Salt Lake City, Utah
Binding and Media Coating:
Mountain States Bindery,
Salt Lake City, Utah
Typeface: Monotype Bodoni
Paper: 80 lb. Warrenflo Book,
Gloss White
Cover: 10 point Springhill Cover,
White